THE BURDEN OF GOVERNMENT

THE BURDEN OF GOVERNMENT

EDWIN S. MILLS

HOOVER INSTITUTION PRESS

STANFORD UNIVERSITY

STANFORD, CALIFORNIA

Hoover Press Publication 328

Copyright 1986 by the Board of Trustees of the
  Leland Stanford Junior University

First printing, 1986

Manufactured in the United States of America

90 89 88 87 86   9 8 7 6 5 4 3 2 1

Library of Congress Cataloging in Publication Data

Mills, Edwin S.
  The burden of government.

  Bibliography: p.
  Includes index.
  1. Economic policy. I. Title.
HD87.M55 1986   338.9   86-211
ISBN 0-8179-8281-7

Design by P. Kelley Baker

Contents

List of Tables
and Figure

Preface

This book represents my thoughts, accumulated over many years, on one of the most important social issues of every era, including our own. Although the subject is surrounded by intemperate controversy, there can be no doubt that the social efficiency, equity, innovativeness, flexibility, and growth of economies depend on ways governments relate to economic activity. Whatever governments may or may not be able to do to promote the achievement of economic goals, it is patent that sufficiently bad governments can prevent such progress. This book explores carefully what governments should and should not do to achieve desirable economic goals.

The book covers an enormous range of intellectual issues. Its goal is to present a coherent and appropriate thread of analysis. To keep the important issues in focus and the book short and readable, many important, detailed issues and facts have been omitted. Once the basic ideas are understood, they can be applied to many issues.

Included is a lengthy Bibliography. The diversity of the material covered inevitably implies that I understand some subjects and their related literatures better than others. I apologize in advance for inevitable slights to important contributions.

The book can be read and understood by anyone who has had one or two undergraduate economics courses. However, a critical reading of some parts of Chapters 3 and 9 requires a much deeper understanding of economics.

I am deeply indebted to my colleagues Richard E. Quandt, Harvey S. Rosen, and Hugo Sonnenschein, who have read drafts of several chapters. I am also indebted to anonymous referees who commented on the penultimate draft of the book. Norma Morris patiently and carefully typed several drafts of the entire book.

I am indebted to the Hoover Institution for financial assistance in writing the book.

ONE

Introduction

This book is concerned with economic analysis of the many roles governments play in contemporary societies. Fundamental, but nontechnical, economic theory is employed to analyze what governments should and should not do, as well as why they do what they do. Basic and long-run matters, rather than day-to-day economic or political issues, provide the framework. Considerable use is made of long-term historical trends and of more contemporary, post–World War II data. But detailed historical data are not the main focus. Such data are squeezed through the filter of economic analysis to provide insights into ways that societies function and how they might function better.

It is important in all economic discussions, particularly for those in this book, to distinguish between positive and normative (welfare) economics. Positive economics concerns explanations of economic phenomena. Normative, or welfare, economics concerns evaluations of the desirability of economic performance and institutions and of government actions. Explanations of economic phenomena require theories of behavior of economic agents, such as producers and consumers, as well as data and statistical methods to estimate behavioral relationships and to test theories. Normative analysis requires a criterion for evaluating economic phenomena so that one knows which economic performance, institutions, or government actions are better than others. Normative economics builds on positive economics and requires accurate positive models of economic behavior.

Although the book contains no technical analysis, it does require a firm grasp of some important propositions in normative economics and of the positive economics that underlies it. Therefore, this chapter reviews findings of normative economics that have been developed during more than two centuries of research by some of the best minds in the economics profession. The purpose is not to repeat textbook analyses but rather to state, with just enough argument to make them clear and plausible, results that will be drawn upon in subsequent chapters. Although much of the book is controversial, the results stated here have been proven carefully and are widely accepted by economists.

SOME NOTES ON WELFARE ECONOMICS

Most of this book is about what private groups can do better than governments and what governments can do better than private groups. Welfare economics is the foundation of such analysis, and this section presents some basic ideas from welfare economics that are important for this book. More detailed and technical accounts of the subject are available in textbooks.[1]

The foundation of welfare economics is economists' measure of people's well-being, or as economists prefer, welfare. When economists say that a person is better off or has more well-being or welfare in situation X than in situation Y, they mean simply that the person prefers X to Y and chooses X if both X and Y are available.[2] That is what will be meant throughout this book. Economists almost always assume that people have complete and consistent preferences. *Completeness* means that people know whether they prefer X to Y for any pair of X and Y situations. Rational choices can be made only among situations about which people have complete preferences. *Consistency* means that if people prefer situation X to Y and Y to Z, then they also prefer X to Z. Consistency is crucial to the notion of coherent preferences.

Assumptions of complete and consistent preferences are unexceptionable as a foundation for a theory of rational or sensible behavior. It is difficult to imagine how a theory of rational goal seeking could be constructed without them. Of course, like any theory of human behavior, the economists' theory is, at best, an approximation. People tend to have complete preferences only among situations similar to those within their experience or their practical range of choice. They have little incentive to undertake the psychic or monetary cost of finding out enough about other situations to have complete preferences. Likewise, experiments have shown that people make inconsistent choices if faced with many options that differ only slightly from each other. More important, certain people, especially children and some infirm adults, are incompetent to judge their preferences, and special provisions must be made for them.

Although these caveats are important, they do not detract from the great importance of how economists view people's behavior. They invariably assume that economic and political behavior is oriented toward coherent goals. An enormous body of evidence supports this assumption in its broad and relevant sense. Furthermore, if the theory were not a good approximation of economic and political behavior, it really would not make much difference to people whether economic and political systems functioned well or badly. In fact, it is not clear that those terms can be given useful meaning outside the framework of the theory of rational behavior. Few people who doubt the truth of economists' assumptions about rational behavior are willing to face this logical consequence of their doubts.

The situations that are the objects of choice have different content in different applications. In the theory of consumer behavior, the relevant situations are sets of quantities of commodities and services (hereafter referred to as *commodities*) that people might buy and consume. Sometimes, *situation* is interpreted more broadly to include not only commodities but also time devoted to work to earn income that can be used to buy commodities. In this book, *situation* will sometimes also include commodities (usually services), such as education and national security, that are provided by governments. Likewise, *situation* will sometimes mean commodities consumed; at other times, it will mean work effort. People have preferences, not only among commodities and work effort at given times but also on how consumption and work are distributed through time.

In any given context, people must make choices among situations available to them. Choices are constrained by earning capacity and prices, by the number of hours in a day, and in other ways. The set of situations available to a person in a given context is referred to as the person's *opportunity set*. In consumer behavior theory, the opportunity set is the set of commodity bundles that cost no more than the consumer's income, perhaps adjusted for other sources of money, such as savings or gifts.

If people choose their preferred situation from those in their opportunity set, they are said to be rational. Rationality, as used here, does not imply selfishness or materialistic preferences. I may deprive myself for the benefit of my children or of waifs down the street or I may spend most of my income on symphonies and nevertheless be rational.

It is common but unjustified to scoff at the notion that people are rational in the broadest sense. Sometimes people say someone is irrational when they mean they disapprove of consumption bundles that were chosen, as when a poor family goes on an expensive vacation. That is a moral concept of irrationality and is not relevant here. It is more relevant to say people are irrational because their consumption choices are not in their long-run interest. For example, people say that heavy cigarette smokers are irrational because they fail to evaluate rationally the resulting danger to their health.

Decisions, such as whether to smoke and choice of marriage partners, with consequences that stretch over decades, place the greatest strain on people's rationality. Beyond doubt, taking rational account of the long-run consequences of decisions is a skill that varies greatly among people.

Both the examples just given and the general issue are important practical problems. Actions and proposed actions of governments are frequently justified by the claim that governments know people's preferences better than people do themselves. Both examples are relevant. Belief that people are irrational when they decide to smoke cigarettes leads governments to tax cigarettes heavily and leads to proposals that governments control cigarette smoking in various ways. Likewise, concern about divorce rates leads to proposals that governments change the legal rules about marriage and divorce—by making marriage more difficult, for example.

The claim that governments possess better information than people about their preferences or about effects of their decisions on themselves is never a legitimate reason for governments to intervene with people's choice. If, for whatever reason, governments possess superior information, the implication is that governments should make the information available to the people, who can then make whatever use of the information they wish in their decision making.

This argument applies to only a limited set of government interventions that are motivated by belief that governments know people's preferences better than people do. Even though this is not a legitimate reason for governments to intervene to control behavior, there may be many reasons that private behavior does not lead to resource allocation that would enable people to be as well off as possible. If so, there may be methods by which governments can intervene to make people better off. This is a complex subject and is, indeed, the subject of this book.

Just as economists assume that consumers behave rationally to further their well-being, so they assume that asset owners have the same goals. Whereas consumers are assumed to care not only about commodities they can consume but also about the kinds and amounts of work they do, asset owners are assumed to care only about the returns to various uses of their property. Thus economists assume that asset owners maximize the returns to their assets, or profits. The assumption that owners maximize returns on their assets is the foundation of the theory of the firm. In order to maximize profits, firms must employ inputs that minimize the costs of given production volumes and must produce quantities and sell at prices that maximize profits (the excess of revenues over costs).

The assumption that firms, or asset owners, are profit maximizers (at least in the long run) is less controversial than the assumption that consumers are utility or well-being maximizers. People accept the assumption that the reason for accumulating assets is to obtain a return from their use, and asset owners thus obtain the largest return possible.

In welfare economics, a distinction is made between social efficiency and equity goals of economic activity. An economy is said to be socially efficient, or is on the utility frontier, if productive resources are allocated so no other allocation can make one or more people better off without making other people worse off. *Social efficiency* means that society is making the best use of its resources to make people as well off as possible, but without regard to the distribution of well-being among people.[3] The notion of the utility frontier is a useful characterization of social efficiency because it is literal: a situation is on the utility frontier if no other situation permits one person to achieve a higher utility number without another person achieving a lower utility number. Thus the term *utility frontier* is used frequently in subsequent chapters. Economists say that resource allocation, or the income distribution, is equitable if it is just or fair according to some criterion. What governments should and should not do to promote social efficiency is discussed in Chapter 3. Similar questions regarding equity are considered in Chapter 4.

Social efficiency is to be contrasted with private efficiency. A firm, for example, is privately efficient if it employs resources so as to maximize its profit. Textbooks show that a privately efficient monopolist is, nevertheless, socially inefficient. It could increase production and sell the extra production at a sufficiently lower price so that customers whose well-being is thereby improved could compensate the firm's owners for their reduced profit. Social efficiency requires that producers and consumers be privately rational, but private rationality does not imply social efficiency.

The utility numbers, or well-being, that people can attain in a socially efficient economy are constrained by available production opportunities.

Available production opportunities depend on the numbers, experience, and training of workers; on the amounts and kinds of natural resources available; on the kinds and amounts of produced or man-made capital available, including structures, machinery, and inventories; and on knowledge of production and distribution technologies. There are many more constraints, and they are much more binding in the short run than in the long run. Within a year, a society's labor force, capital stock (buildings, machinery, and the like), natural resources, and technology are almost immutable. Within a decade, many things can be changed. Within 20 to 50 years, almost the entire capital stock and labor force are replaced, technology can be revolutionized, and so forth. During the 35-year period from 1945 to 1980, Japan went from living standards at about subsistence levels to living standards that were among the highest in the world. In both 1945 and 1980, Japan was almost certainly close to its utility frontier, given its short-run constraints.

Attaining social efficiency is extremely important. People care more about their living standards than about almost anything else, and governments do many things that affect living standards or utilities. For example, during a period as short as a year or so, government may be able to take actions that reduce involuntary unemployment by a few percent of the labor force. That would permit a sizeable move toward the utility frontier. Alternatively, during a similar period, government might be able to reduce the inflation rate from 10 to 5 percent, permitting prices to be better signals for desirable resource allocation.

During longer periods, much more can be done. The rate at which short-run constraints are relaxed, permitting the utility frontier to move outward and well-being to rise, depends on how resources are allocated. Saving and investment cause the capital stock to grow, research and many other actions promote new technology, and education and experience improve labor productivity. Appropriate government actions that enable economic growth to correspond to people's preferences for present versus future consumption can make a great difference to social efficiency within a decade or so. Thus, achievement of social efficiency encompasses issues related to economic growth as well as issues related to resource allocation within short-run constraints. All of these issues of short- and long-run social efficiency are given meaning by the assumption that people's behavior is rational.

Social efficiency is a relatively objective concept. In principle and—at least in most cases and after considerable research—in practice, it is possible to say with confidence what government actions permit the economy to attain the utility frontier. Equity is a subjective concept. What one person considers an equitable income distribution, another considers inequitable. Nevertheless, it will be shown in Chapter 4 that welfare economics has many valuable things to say about government actions to promote equity.

Starting more than two centuries ago, economists have written hundreds of books and articles on the social efficiency of private markets. In each generation, some of the best minds in the profession have turned their attention to this issue. There is, by now, remarkable agreement on basic aspects of the subject.

Consumers choose consumption and employment situations that make them as well off as possible, given prices they must pay, their earning power, and other constraints. That is, they choose the preferred bundle of commodities from their opportunity set. Firm owners make themselves as well off as possible by obtaining the greatest return possible from assets they have to invest in firms. This leads them to maximize profit from whatever set of products they produce. It also leads asset owners to invest their property in lines of production that are as profitable as any that can be found, and that leads to movement of capital to production of commodities where profit is greater than elsewhere. Thus the self-interest of property owners leads them to move assets to production of products that consumers value, as indicated by prices they are willing to pay. Likewise, the desire of most workers to obtain high living standards induces them to offer their services where returns to their work are high. Thus they are led to produce commodities that are most desired by consumers.

Much more careful formulation of these ideas leads to the most remarkable theory economists have produced: Provided that technology permits competitive markets to exist and to price characteristics of production and consumption that affect people's well-being, then a market system in which people are free to allocate their labor as they wish, to accumulate and allocate assets in pursuit of profit, and to spend their incomes as they wish generates competitive markets and resource allocation that place the economy on the utility frontier.[4]

This is not only the most important result economics has ever produced but also the cornerstone of much that economists have had to say about actions governments should and should not take to ensure social efficiency of the economy. An important issue is what conditions technology must satisfy to permit competitive markets to exist and to generate socially efficient resource allocation. There is disagreement and confusion among economists about the role of technology in society.

Most economists would say that if technology results in scale economies, that permit only one producer, or perhaps a few producers, in a market, then competition cannot exist and private markets cannot be socially efficient without government intervention. Likewise, most economists would say that if production causes polluting discharges that damage people's health, then technology does not permit competitive markets to value this aspect of production, even though it affects people's well-being. Again, the conclusion is that private markets cannot generate social efficiency without government intervention. An important purpose of this book, carried out in Chapter 3, is to show that most economists place too narrow an interpretation on the conditions that private markets must satisfy in order to be able to generate social efficiency.

One other characteristic of competitive markets is important in providing a link between social efficiency and equity issues. A characteristic that permits competitive markets to be socially efficient is that competitive equilibrium prices represent social opportunity costs (the value people place on production foregone in order to produce a certain commodity). If tomatoes cost 50¢ per pound, it means that the inputs, priced on competitive input markets, needed to produce one pound of tomatoes in the cheapest way possible, could produce 50¢ worth of other commodities foregone to produce the tomatoes. Likewise, a plumber who earns $20 per hour repairing plumbing could have earned $20 per hour doing other equally onerous work, such as installing plumbing in new buildings. It is the fact that competitive prices reflect opportunity costs that enables competitive markets to allocate resources to uses that are most valuable to consumers and hence that permits a competitive economy to achieve the utility frontier. Competitive profits are the returns to assets that are needed to induce people to forego current consumption so some part of production can be invested to produce commodities in the future. Competitive profits also reflect opportunity costs and are just as important in generating socially efficient amounts and uses of assets as competitive wages are in generating socially efficient amounts and uses of labor.

These competitive output and input prices not only provide a socially efficient allocation of inputs and outputs but also generate both incomes to input owners and an associated income distribution. The resulting income distribution depends on the distribution of natural abilities, education, skills, experience, man-made capital, and valuable natural resources. Education, skills, and experience are collectively referred to as *human capital*, and man-made capital and valuable natural resources are referred to as *physical capital*. Thus one can say that the income distribution generated by competitive markets depends on the ownership distribution of human and physical capital. In the short run, amounts of human and physical capital are fixed. But in the long run, they respond to prices. High wages for engineers, lawyers, or plumbers induce people to enter those occupations. High returns to capital in manufacturing electronic chips induce asset owners to move their assets, and savers to move their savings, into that industry. Thus associated with a competitive equilibrium, and with a distribution of ownership of human and physical capital, is a set of prices and quantities that generates a distribution of income. This will be referred to as the *competitive distribution of income*. A key question is whether a competitive income distribution is also equitable and, if not, how it can be redistributed to make it equitable. These issues are discussed in Chapter 4.

SCOPE OF THE BOOK

The preceding provided the briefest outline of welfare economics. Although it is abstract and sometimes arid, it is the only coherent framework known by which to evaluate how well an economy satisfies people's needs and wants. And it is the only coherent framework known by which to evaluate what governments should and should not do to ensure social efficiency and equity. It underlies the analysis in this book.

This book is concerned with normative and positive analysis of roles of government in domestic economies. It seems patent that national governments must represent their citizens in relating to other national governments. Exactly what the international activities of governments should be is at least as controversial and intellectually difficult to analyze as governments' domestic roles. However, international issues are beyond the scope of this book. Specifically, I make no comments on roles of governments in providing national security or in other relationships with national governments elsewhere.

The content of the book is as follows. Chapter 2 lays out the factual background regarding growth of governments during the late nineteenth and twentieth centuries. It is positive, indeed descriptive, in character. Although a brief account of growth of governments in some other countries is provided, attention is focused on governments in the United States. I outline growth of both federal and state and local governments, indicating growth of spending by function and growth of regulatory activities. Chapters 3 through 8 are normative in character, with Chapters 3 and 4 the conceptual heart of the book. Chapter 3 pursues the analysis of social efficiency introduced earlier in this chapter and analyzes government actions to enable the economy to achieve the utility frontier. Chapter 4 analyzes equity notions and proposes government actions to improve equity in the United States. Chapters 5 through 7 explore specific areas of government activity. Chapter 5 analyzes appropriate national government macroeconomic policies in the light of the conclusions of Chapters 3 and 4. Chapters 6 and 7 analyze regulatory actions of both federal and state and local governments. Chapter 8 discusses roles of governments of poor countries. Chapter 9 uses positive economic analysis to explore why governments are so much larger and more intrusive than they need be to enable the economy to be socially efficient and equitable. Chapter 10 presents some concluding comments.

The statement that Chapters 3 through 8 are normative means that they are directed at answering the question: Assuming that governments are motivated to achieve social efficiency and equity, what should they do? Thus in these chapters, governments are assumed, without question, to have the motivations implied by welfare economics. The conclusions drawn in these chapters indicate that governments do many things that interfere with both social efficiency and equity. Chapter 9 employs positive economic analysis to explore why governments fail to pursue social efficiency and equity.

TWO

The Growth of Governments

Whatever else can be said, governments have been the greatest growth sector of the last century in virtually all high-income countries. However it is measured, growth of governments has outstripped that of other rapidly growing sectors, such as private services.

This chapter traces the historical growth of governments, beginning with a comparison of growth in five industrialized countries during the hundred years stretching from 1880 to 1980 and then focusing in greater detail on growth of government within the United States. As positive economic history, it provides important factual background for the normative analysis presented in Chapters 3 through 8 and for the positive analysis in Chapter 9.

GOVERNMENT GROWTH IN INDUSTRIALIZED COUNTRIES, 1880–1980

The data here are for Germany (West Germany after World War II), Japan, Sweden, the United Kingdom, and the United States. These countries were selected partly because data were readily available for both national income and government expenditure and also because these five are among the world's most industrialized and highest income countries.

Table 1 shows government spending as a percent of gross national product (GNP) for the five countries at twenty-year intervals from 1880 to 1980. All government spending—national, state or provincial, and local—is included.[1] In some cases, to avoid the greatest effects of the two world wars, years other than 1920 and 1940 have been included.

The data in Table 1 show that all five governments were small in 1880. Indeed, 1880 may approximate the time when governments' GNP shares were smallest in these countries.[2] In that year, their average spending was less than 8 percent of their countries' total output or income. Only in Japan did governments spend more than 10 percent of GNP. By 1980, government spending was more than half of GNP in Sweden, more than 40 percent in Germany and the United Kingdom, and about one-third in the United States. Only in Japan was it below 30 percent.

Growth of government spending as a share of GNP has been steady and pervasive in these five countries during the twentieth century. In none of them did government spending shrink relative to GNP during any twenty-year period covered by the table. In most periods it grew. The table also makes clear that growth of governments' GNP shares did not result just from its inexorable increase during the two world wars and a failure to shrink after the wars. In most of the five countries, governments' shares of GNP grew during the decades between the two wars and during the decades after World War II.

TABLE 1   PERCENTAGE OF GOVERNMENT SPENDING
             IN GNP: GERMANY, JAPAN, SWEDEN, THE
             UNITED KINGDOM, AND THE UNITED
             STATES, 1880–1980 (Calendar Years)

	Germany	Japan	Sweden	United Kingdom	United States
1880	3	12	6	10	8
1900	6	16	6	10	8
1920	8[a]	16	8	23[d]	13
1940	12[b]	21[c]	12	23[e]	18
1960	15	21	24	30	27
1980	43	25	57	42	33

SOURCES: 1880–1960 data are from Sam Peltzman, "The Growth of Government," *Journal of Law and Economics* 23, no. 2 (October 1980):209–88. 1980 data are from Organization for Economic Cooperation and Development, *National Accounts Statistics, 1968–1980* (Paris: OECD, 1982).

[a]1925   [b]1935   [c]1930   [d]1922   [e]1938

The most striking characteristic of the data in Table 1 is the similarity of government growth among the five countries. In all of them, governments were a small share of GNP a century ago and are now a large share. It seems nearly certain that basic and similar forces have been at work to cause government growth in all five countries and that factors peculiar to one or two countries are not important explanations. Nevertheless, there are differences. In 1880 Japan, governments were a larger share of GNP than in other countries, and Japanese governments grew less during the century covered by the table. In 1980, Japanese and U.S. governments were smaller shares of GNP than were governments in the other three countries.

It is important to appreciate the magnitude of government growth implied by the data in Table 1. In the United States of 1980, for example, government spending was four times as great a share of GNP as it was a century earlier. In all five countries, GNP grew rapidly during most of the century. In the United States, real GNP per capita grew at a compound rate somewhat less than 2 percent per year, on the average, during the century. But real government spending grew more than 5 percent per year, on the average. Population grew a little less than 1.4 percent per year. These figures imply that real government spending per capita grew about twice as fast as real income and output per capita during the century.[3] The accounting implication is that disposable income grew considerably less rapidly than personal income. This is aside from any economic effect the growth of government may have had in slowing the growth of total output or income.

By about 1980, in most industrialized countries, government spending absorbed between 25 and 50 percent of the economy's total output or income. During the century between 1880 and 1980, government spending grew from a few percent of GNP to those extraordinarily large sizes. It would be difficult to imagine an intellectually more intriguing or practically more important subject than understanding the reasons for such growth and the extent to which it is justified by social efficiency and equity considerations.

GOVERNMENT SPENDING
IN THE UNITED STATES

In recent years, governments in the United States have spent about one-third of the country's total output or income. How do governments spend such huge sums? How much is spent by each level of government and for what purposes? To answer these questions, we will trace total, federal, and state and local government spending, concentrating on the period from 1960 to the early 1980s.

Total Government Spending

Table 2 shows both total spending by all governments—federal, state, and local—in the United States and the percentage breakdown by function for 1960, 1970, 1980, and 1981.

The top line of Table 2 shows that total government spending in 1981 was 7.3 times its 1960 level. The 1981 consumer price index was 3.07 times its 1960 level, so real government expenditures in 1981 were 2.4

TABLE 2   TOTAL GOVERNMENT EXPENDITURES AND
             PERCENTAGE DISTRIBUTION BY FUNCTION
             (Fiscal Years)

	1960	*1970*	*1980*	*1981*
Total expenditures (millions of dollars)	151,288	332,985	958,657	1,109,815
Percent distribution by function				
National defense and international relations	32.3	25.3	15.6	15.7
Space research and technology	0.3	1.1	0.5	0.5
Postal service	2.5	2.3	1.9	1.8
Education	12.8	16.7	15.0	14.2
Social services and income maintenance	9.3	11.5	13.1	12.7
Transportation	7.7	5.2	4.3	4.1
Public safety	2.5	2.6	3.1	3.0
Environment and housing	7.1	6.0	7.1	7.1
Government administration	2.2	2.3	2.5	2.3
Interest on government debt	6.2	5.5	7.9	8.8
Public utilities	2.7	2.3	3.5	3.6
Liquor store expenditures	0.7	0.5	0.3	0.2
Insurance trust expenditures	11.6	14.6	20.8	21.5
Other	2.1	4.1	4.4	4.5
Total	100.0	100.0	100.0	100.0

SOURCE: Tax Foundation, Inc., *Facts and Figures on Government Finance* (Washington, D.C.: Tax Foundation, 1983, Tables 7 and 8).

times their 1960 level. The U.S. population grew only 27 percent during the same period, so most of the growth of government spending was per capita growth. Real GNP in 1981 was 2.05 times its 1960 level, so real government spending grew much faster than real income or output. As a result, governments' share of GNP grew from 27 percent in 1960 to about 37 percent in 1981. These figures show rapid growth of U.S. governments during the 21-year period, by worldwide or historical standards in comparison with other industrialized countries or with U.S. history.

The remainder of Table 2 shows the percent breakdown of total government spending by conventional categories. The first category, national defense and international relations, includes the spending by the departments of Defense and State, the intelligence agencies, and small parts of spending by many other federal agencies. The remaining categories represent domestic spending and are the subject of this book. The "Other" category at the bottom of the table includes a variety of relatively small spending programs.

The primary lesson of the data in Table 2 is that the share of defense and international relations spending has declined dramatically and the share of domestic spending has risen. In 1980 and 1981, spending for defense and international relations was less than half the share of total government spending it was in 1960. Real spending for defense and international relations was little more in 1981 than in 1960. Thus the popular view that large government spending is mostly for national defense and other international purposes is dramatically and increasingly wrong. Virtually the entire growth of governments since 1960 has been for domestic purposes. Furthermore, the shares of domestic programs that represent traditional government responsibilities have declined. These include the postal service, transportation, public safety, public utilities, and some parts of the environment and housing category. Although the shares of some programs in these categories have grown, their total share has declined during the 21-year period. Education is also a traditional government responsibility. Its share of total government spending increased until the 1970s, but has declined since, as the postwar baby boom has worked its way through the educational system.

Most of the growth in spending shares is in insurance trust expenditures and in social services and income maintenance. These categories include the important programs that provide transfer payments (payments made without an obligation to provide commodities or services to the government) to people. They are discussed in Chapter 4. Many programs in these categories did not exist in the 1950s; others were very small. They represent government provision of money or services to an enormous variety of groups of people. Most government transfer programs to individuals (totaling about 11 percent of GNP or one-third of government spending in the early 1980s) are in this category.

The final category whose government-spending share has increased substantially is interest payments on government debt. Its share has increased partly because deficits have increased the debt and partly because interest rates on the debt have risen (mostly because of the rapid inflation) since the early 1970s. The federal government has had much larger deficits and therefore much larger debt and interest payments on it than state and local governments who, unlike the federal government, have their deficit financing limited by their laws and constitutions. Federal deficit spending is discussed in Chapters 5 and 9.

I turn now to the distribution of spending among the three levels of U.S. governments: federal, state, and local. Table 3 shows total spending by all governments and its percent distribution among the three levels at about decade intervals from 1902 to 1982, excluding 1942 because of the effects of World War II. Before proceeding, it should be noted that an important issue is the presentation of intergovernmental transfers. During recent years, the federal government has transferred large sums to state and local governments for many purposes. Such transfers were only $7 million in 1902, rose to $1 billion in 1946 (at the end of World War II) and to $10 billion in the early 1960s, and were more than $90 billion in 1981. In the early 1980s, federal transfers were about 20 percent of total

TABLE 3   TOTAL GOVERNMENT SPENDING AND
              SHARES OF FEDERAL, STATE, AND LOCAL
              GOVERNMENTS, 1902–1982 (Fiscal Years)

	TOTAL GOVERNMENT EXPENDITURE (MILLIONS OF DOLLARS)	PERCENTAGE SHARES		
		Federal	State	Local
1902	1,660	34.5	10.8	54.8
1913	3,215	30.2	11.6	58.3
1922	9,297	40.5	13.6	46.0
1932	12,437	34.3	20.6	45.1
1952	99,847	71.7	13.4	15.0
1962	176,240	64.4	16.6	19.1
1972	399,098	60.7	20.3	19.0
1982	1,196,897	65.7	19.2	15.1

SOURCE: Tax Foundation, Inc., *Facts and Figures on Government Finance* (Washington, D.C.: Tax Foundation, 1983, Tables 9 and 10).

revenues of state and local governments. In Table 3, such transfers are included in the federal share.[4]

The key trend portrayed in Table 3 is the growth of federal and state shares of total government spending and the shrinkage of the local government share. In 1902, local government spending was more than half of total government spending, and transfers from federal and state governments to local governments were negligible. In 1982, local government spending was only 15 percent of total government spending. During the 80-year period, federal and state governments have both nearly doubled their shares of total government spending. The growth of total government spending, shown in the second column of Table 3, has been so rapid that even local governments have increased their spending during the twentieth century. The data in Table 3 imply that local government spending was almost 200 times as great in 1982 as in 1902. The 1982 price level was about 10 times its 1902 value, so real local government was almost 20 times as great in 1982 as in 1902. It is by no means obvious why the share of local governments in total government spending should have fallen so much. That subject is pursued in Chapter 9.

As Table 3 implies, federal and state government spending have grown much more than local government spending during the twentieth century. In 1982, federal government spending was almost 1,400 times its 1902 level. State government spending was almost 1,300 times as great in 1982 as in 1902. Real federal and state government spending were more than 100 times as great in 1982 as in 1902. No important part of the private sector of the economy comes close to matching these growth rates.

Federal Government Spending

Table 4 shows total federal government spending for 1960, 1970, and 1980 and the shares of spending by broad functions. The expenditure figures include grants to state and local governments. The revenue sharing function is entirely such grants, but other functions include amounts paid to state and local governments for purposes shown. The offsetting-receipts function is mainly federal government contributions to employee pensions, which are paid to a trust fund operated by the federal government.

The top line of Table 4 reflects the rapid growth of federal government spending during the twenty-year period. Federal government spending was more than 6 times as great in 1980 as in 1960. In 1980, the price level was 2.8 times its 1960 level, so real federal government spending doubled during those two decades.

TABLE 4   TOTAL FEDERAL GOVERNMENT
               EXPENDITURES AND SHARES BY FUNCTION,
               1960–1980 (Fiscal Years)

	1960	1970	1980
Total expenditures			
(billions of dollars)	92.2	195.7	576.7
Shares			
National defense	49.0	40.2	23.6
International affairs	3.3	2.2	1.9
Income security	19.8	22.0	33.5
Health	0.9	6.2	9.6
Veterans benefits and services	5.9	4.4	3.7
Education, training, employment	1.1	4.4	5.3
Commerce and housing credit	1.7	1.1	1.4
Transportation	4.4	3.6	3.7
Natural resources and environment	1.7	1.6	2.4
Energy	0.5	0.5	1.1
Community and regional development	0.2	1.2	1.8
Agriculture	2.8	2.6	0.8
Interest	9.0	9.4	11.2
Revenue sharing	0.2	0.3	1.5
General science, space, technology	0.7	2.3	1.0
General government	1.1	1.0	0.8
Administration of justice	0.4	0.5	0.8
Offsetting receipts	− 2.7	− 3.4	− 3.8

SOURCE: U.S. Census Bureau, *Statistical Abstract of the United States 1982–83* (Washington, D.C.: U.S. Government Printing Office, 1984, Table 421).

As with the total government expenditure data in Table 2, the crucial trend shown in Table 4 is the large decrease in the shares of the military and international categories, with corresponding increases in shares of domestic spending. Military and international spending in 1980 was less than half the share of total federal spending that it had been in 1960. The income security, health and education, and other similar functions have shown the most rapidly rising shares. These are nontraditional federal government functions that hardly existed before about 1950. They include transfers and direct service provision to large and diverse groups of people. Most of the important federal programs that are transfers to individuals are in these categories. Most traditional federal domestic functions, such as natural resource management and highway construction, are small and declining shares of spending.

State and Local Government Spending

Table 5 shows total state and local government spending for 1960, 1970, and 1980 and shares for a classification of functions similar to that employed in previous tables. It makes little sense to separate state and local government spending by function. Functions performed or financed by state governments in some states are performed or financed by local governments in others. It should also be mentioned that expenditures shown in Table 5 include those financed by revenues received by state and local governments from the federal government. Thus federal transfers to state and local governments are counted as expenditures in both Tables 4 and 5. As a result, the sum of expenditures in the two tables exceeds the total shown for all governments in Table 2 by the amounts of such transfers. Finally, it should be indicated that the insurance trust expenditure function consists of state and local government employee pension expenditures and unemployment compensation, both of which are paid from trust funds.

TABLE 5   TOTAL STATE AND LOCAL GOVERNMENT
              EXPENDITURES AND SHARES BY FUNCTION,
              1960–1980 (Fiscal Years)

	1960	1970	1980
Total expenditures (billions of dollars)	61.0	148.1	432.3
Shares			
Education	36.1	40.1	36.3
Highways	18.2	12.5	9.1
Public welfare	8.5	11.2	12.4
Health and hospitals	7.5	7.4	8.8
Police protection and correction	3.6	4.7	5.4
Natural resources	2.3	2.1	1.5
Sanitation and sewerage	3.3	2.6	3.6
Housing and urban renewal	1.7	1.6	1.7
Interest	3.2	3.3	4.0
Utilities and liquor stores	5.6	6.3	8.4
Insurance trust expenditures	4.4	4.9	6.7
Other	5.6	3.3	2.1

SOURCE: U.S. Census Bureau, *Statistical Abstract of the United States 1982–83* (Washington, D.C.: U.S. Government Printing Office, 1984, Tables 473 and 475).

The top line of Table 5 shows the rapid growth of state and local government spending during the two-decade period. State and local government spending was 7.1 times as great in 1980 as in 1960. As was mentioned earlier, the price level was 2.8 times as great in 1980 as in 1960, so real state and local government spending was 2.5 times as great in 1980 as in 1960. The only function whose share shows a large decrease in Table 5 is highway expenditures, which dropped by 50 percent during the two decades. The largest single increase in the table is in the share of public welfare. It is the major category of transfer payments to individuals that is paid by state and local governments. Part, however, is funded by grants from the federal government.

Table 5 does not show that growth of state and local government expenditures has been concentrated in a few functions the way Table 4 did for the federal government. Mainly, the reason is the absence from Table 5 of expenditures for military and international purposes. That share showed the major decline in the federal spending table, and it is entirely a federal function. State and local government spending increases have been distributed over a broader range of functions than federal government spending increases.

EXAMPLES OF GOVERNMENT
SPENDING PROGRAMS

The summary data that have been presented here do not begin to convey the complexity and variety of government activites. The federal government budget is a volume the size of a large city's telephone directory. No single individual understands the true workings and effects of more than a few of the spending and regulatory programs it includes. State government budgets vary in size but are much more difficult to understand than the federal government budget. The federal government budget presents summary data by categories that are meaningful for perspective and analysis whereas most state government budgets are in categories laid out in particular laws. Meaningful survey categories, such as those in Table 5, are put together by the U.S. Census Bureau. It is almost impossible to compare budgets of different state governments. Similar comments hold for local government budgets.

It would require years of work and a large volume to give an adequate summary of all the important government spending and regulatory programs in the United States. In fact, government spending and regulation affect virtually every aspect of citizens' lives and business activity. Many spending and regulatory programs are enormously complex and detailed, evidently designed to accomplish very specific goals. Analyzing what such purposes are and whether they are justified is the overall purpose of this book. The following discussion is designed to illustrate the scope and complexity of government actions with a few examples. The number of potential examples is almost endless.

Federal Lending Programs

Most government spending is for direct acquisition of commodities or for transfer payments. However, the federal government has a wide variety of programs under which it either lends money or guarantees loans made by the private sector to people or institutions. Although the amounts of such loans are very large and annual federal expenditure on them is many billions of dollars, their complexity is their hallmark.

Table 6 shows dollar amounts of direct and guaranteed loans outstanding in 1982 under the large programs then in existence. Primary headings are federal agencies that administer the programs. Subheadings refer to specific programs.

The two programs under funds appropriated to the president are military and civilian foreign aid. The Department of Agriculture administers several large programs. Most of the large sums are in loan guarantee programs. The Commodity Credit Corporation program, one of the largest direct loan programs in the table, is the government's program to raise agricultural prices above market levels. The government achieves the goal by making loans to farmers to keep crops off the market. Loans are repaid only if crop prices are high. The Public Law 480 program is part of the foreign aid program. The Rural Electrification Administration is a federal agency established in the 1930s to electrify farms. To this end, it borrows money on markets, and its debts are guaranteed by the government. The programs under the Commerce Department are for regional development assistance and for oceanic and atmospheric research and development. The large sums under Education are for many programs and include direct and guaranteed loans to college students. Under Health and Human Services, the government makes and guarantees loans for such things as hospital equipment. Large sums appear under Housing and Urban Development. They include programs of mortgage guarantees for homeowners and for the government's purchase of mortgages in the secondary mortgage market, as well as loans made or guaranteed for low-income housing. Under Interior, programs include direct and guaranteed loans for natural resource development. Under Transportation, the largest sum is for loans to subsidize U.S.-flag merchant shipping. The Treasury programs are two large ad hoc pro-

TABLE 6   OUTSTANDING FEDERAL DIRECT AND
               GUARANTEED LOANS, FISCAL YEAR 1982
               (Millions of Dollars)

	Guaranteed Loans	Direct Loans
Total loans	$547,324	$100,218
Funds appropriated to the president		
International security assistance	11,693	5,922
International development assistance	1,128	12,010
Agriculture:		
Farmers Home Administration		
Agricultural credit	24,544	795
Rural housing	24,989	447
Rural development	9,790	153
Commodity Credit Corporation	2,650	12,484
Public Law 480 long-term export		
credits	—	8,307
Rural Electrification Administration	20,125	—
Commerce:		
Economic Development Administration	632	891
National Oceanic and Atmospheric		
Administration	174	—
Education	27,700	9,859
Energy	2,156	13
Health and Human Services: Health programs	1,542	921
Housing and Urban Development:		
Low-rent public housing	20,770	162
Federal Housing Administration	142,252	—
Government National Mortgage		
Association	115,537	4,074
Other housing programs	—	8,980
Interior	143	441
Transportation:		
Federal ship financing fund	7,176	—
Railroad programs	—	569
Other	2,996	434
Treasury:		
Guarantee of New York City notes	1,444	—
Chrysler Corporation guarantee		
program	1,200	—
Biomass energy development	—	—
NASA: Long-term satellite leases	758	—

TABLE 6 (continued)

	Guaranteed Loans	Direct Loans
Veterans Administration:		
Housing loans and default claims	108,784	1,906
Insurance policy and other loans	—	1,462
District of Columbia	—	1,684
Export-Import Bank	6,069	16,565
Federal Deposit Insurance Corporation	—	705
Federal Home Loan Bank Board	—	758
National Credit Union Administration	106	149
Small Business Administration:		
Business and investment loans	9,947	3,096
Disaster loan fund	11	6,073
Pollution control bond guarantees	306	—
Tennessee Valley Authority	1,258	267
Other agencies and programs	1,444	1,091

SOURCE: Tax Foundation, Inc., *Facts and Figures on Government Finance* (Washington, D.C.: Tax Foundation, 1983, Table 105).

grams, one to prevent bankruptcy of New York City in 1975 and the other to prevent bankruptcy of the Chrysler Corporation in the early 1980s. The NASA program is loan guarantees to develop satellite leasing for commercial purposes. The largest program administered by the Veterans Administration is mortgage guarantees for veterans. The federal government lends money to the District of Columbia government for a variety of purposes. The Export-Import Bank makes and guarantees loans to promote exports and imports. The Federal Deposit Insurance Corporation makes loans to commercial banks that are in financial difficulty. The Federal Home Loan Bank Board makes loans to savings and loan associations. The National Credit Union Administration makes and guarantees loans to credit unions, which make loans to and accept deposits from employees of institutions in which they are located. The Small Business Administration makes and guarantees loans to small businesses. The Tennessee Valley Authority is a federal agency that produces electricity in the Tennessee Valley and nearby areas. The data in

Table 6 exclude a large number of off-budget lending programs. These are programs that receive money from the federal government but that Congress has decided not to include in its budgetary data. Net federal government outlays on off-budget loan programs were about $14 billion in 1982.

Table 6 shows that the federal government had loan guarantees of half a trillion dollars and direct loans of $100 billion outstanding in 1982. The terms of these loans and loan guarantee programs vary enormously from one program to another. Nobody knows the cost of these programs to taxpayers. Some loans are kept on the government's books even though the probability of principle or interest payments is slight. Most loans are made at interest rates well below market. In some cases, default is hidden by new loans used to pay principle or interest on old loans. In some cases, such as the crop price support loans, repayment is contingent on high crop prices. Otherwise, the government ends up with crops it must pay to store, whose market value is problematical, and that, for political reasons, they may never sell.

Each year, Congress appropriates money to support the loan programs, but it is difficult or impossible for many programs to establish what the government loan subsidy amounts are, what default rates are, and how much of current appropriations is to hide de facto default.

The United States has one of the world's most sophisticated, complex, and subtle private financial markets. Private markets can provide loans of incredible complexity and in almost any amount if there is a good prospect of a competitive return. Why, then, should the federal government be involved in such a large number of complex loan programs? It is inconceivable that the federal agencies are able to make risk and return evaluations that private institutions are incapable of making. All the evidence indicates that the returns on federal loan programs are well below those in private financial markets. The answer must be that federal intervention is for the purpose of providing loans at below-market rates of interest to particular groups and for subsidization of such groups and such programs. Why do it with loans or loan guarantees instead of with direct subsidies? Is subsidization justified? Some hints of answers to these questions are provided in later chapters.

Government Transfer Programs

Our discussion here delves somewhat more deeply into government transfer expenditures. Transfers, as was indicated in Chapter 1, are payments made to people because they are thought to be deserving and made without obligation on the recipient to render services or provide commodities. In practice, the distinction is not entirely clear. Sometimes transfer recipients are required to render services, as in work requirements some states have for public welfare recipients (sometimes referred to as *workfare*). Similarly, many government programs to finance service production entail a subsidy element. For example, as discussed earlier, most federal loan programs entail subsidies. Although the subsidies are in the nature of transfer programs, they are not so recorded in the data.

Table 7 shows 1981 spending on transfer payments to persons by all levels of government in the United States and indicates the level of

TABLE 7   GOVERNMENT TRANSFER PROGRAMS TO
            PERSONS, CALENDAR YEAR 1981
            (Billions of Dollars)

Total government transfer payments to persons	323.9
Federal government, total	280.9
From social insurance funds, total	222.8
Old-age, survivors, and disability insurance	138.7
Hospital and medical insurance	43.3
Unemployment insurance	15.2
Railroad retirement	5.3
Federal civilian pensions	18.2
Veterans life insurance	1.3
Workers' compensation	0.9
Military retirement	14.0
Veterans benefits	14.8
Food stamp benefits	10.1
Black lung benefits	1.7
Other	17.5
State and local governments, total	43.0
From social insurance funds, total	20.2
Government pensions	17.0
Cash sickness compensation	0.9
Workers' compensation	2.3
Direct relief	17.0
General assistance	0.9
Aid to families with dependent children	1.5
Other categorical public assistance	2.2
Other	5.8

SOURCE: Tax Foundation, Inc., *Facts and Figures on Government Finance* (Washington, D.C.: Tax Foundation, 1983, Table 28).
NOTE: Figures at each indention sum to the figure immediately above.

government that provided the funds. Some programs, wholly or partly financed by the federal government, are administered by state or local governments. Unlike the loan programs considered previously, government transfer programs are a large part of both total government spending and GNP. In 1981, transfers were one-third of total government spending and 11 percent of GNP.

The largest transfer programs are under Income Security (Table 4) and under Public Welfare (Table 5). As Table 7 shows, the federal government finances about 85 percent of transfer payments to persons. By far, the largest transfer program is old-age, survivors, and disability insurance, which includes social security, medicare, and disability programs. The next biggest program is hospital and medical insurance, which includes medicaid funds. Other large federal programs are unemployment payments and food stamps. Most remaining federal programs are pension and Veterans Administration programs. Among state and local government programs, by far the largest is aid to families with dependent children. It, and the other programs under direct relief, constitutes what are usually referred to as welfare payments.

The programs covered in Table 7 represent extremely large sums of money and have grown more rapidly than any other significant government spending programs during recent years. Total government transfer expenditures were only $25 billion in 1959, 5.2 percent of GNP. Thus transfer spending, as a share of GNP, more than doubled in little more than two decades.

The programs represented in Table 7 are not only large but also varied and complex. Some are transfers of money to people, and some are direct provision of commodities and services, such as food and health services. Some, such as the direct relief programs, are aimed at poor people. Others, such as the social security, veterans, and pension programs, are provided without regard to recipients' income or assets. Furthermore, transfer programs that are not aimed at poor people have grown much faster since 1959 than those that are so focused.

Many transfer programs are extremely complex. Many have complicated eligibility rules and an elaborate bureaucracy to administer them. Many programs permit important elements of discretion in program administration. Some, such as the black lung and other disability programs, have been subjects of extensive litigation between the government and potential beneficiaries.

Why do governments provide transfers? What goals are they trying to accomplish? Why are there so many programs, and why are they so complex? These issues are discussed at length in Chapters 4 and 9.

THREE

Governments and Social Efficiency

This chapter and the next bring welfare economics to bear on the extraordinary growth and size of governments documented in Chapter 2. Government actions to enable the economy to achieve social efficiency are examined here, and government actions to achieve equity are analyzed in Chapter 4. Both chapters assume without question that governments' goals are promotion of social efficiency and equity. Only in Chapter 9 is the question asked why democratic governments' actions provide such poor approximations to those indicated by welfare economic analysis.

It would be an enormous and fruitless task to analyze even a fraction of the many complex government spending programs listed in Chapter 2. They have a great variety of purposes and mechanisms. They were enacted and amended at many different times, by different levels of governments, and in different economic and political conditions. In addition, programs interact in various ways. For example, a frequent justification for a new program is that, if the government is justified in doing *A* for one group, then it must be justified in doing *B* for another group. For example, it is sometimes claimed that if the government can give large transfers to those who do not work, surely it can employ tariffs and quotas to limit imports and thus protect jobs of those who work and pay taxes. As a second example, accomplishment of the goals of one program sometimes requires addition of other programs. New York City has had rent control since World War II. Given that rental housing demand is greater and supply is smaller due to the low rents, government control of rents at levels below equilibrium inevitably produces an excess of rental housing demand over supply. Landlords undermaintain dwellings to keep costs at levels that can be covered by controlled rents. This leads to demands by tenants for legislation to compel landlords to maintain dwellings in specific ways, for legislation to prevent conversion of dwellings from rental to owner-occupancy, and so on.

Such examples are endless. Instead of analyzing sequences of particular, related government activities, this chapter takes a long step back from existing government programs and asks what governments need to do to ensure efficiency of the economy. The goal is to establish principles to employ in evaluating government actions. These principles can then be used to analyze justifications for particular government programs or sets of programs. We use them to analyze specific categories of government activities in subsequent chapters.

GENERAL CHARACTERISTICS
OF GOVERNMENTS

At this point, it is worthwhile to comment on some basic characteristics of governments. The substantive issue of this chapter is the use of welfare economic analysis to infer government actions that enable the economy to employ its productive resources in socially efficient fashion. Such analysis rests on the conception of the nature of governments explained here.

It is assumed throughout the book that sovereign governments are inevitable and desirable. The alternative is anarchy. It is reasonable to define a sovereign government as any institution that has the power to make and enforce rules of human conduct. Anarchy is the absence of such an institution. Political philosophers have understood for centuries that anarchy is not a viable situation. Starting from a state of anarchy, it would be both possible and profitable for some group to establish a sovereign government. It would be possible because an anarchistic society has no means of preventing establishment of a government that has sovereignty over it. The government might be established either from outside the society, say by a sovereign government of another society, or from inside the society, perhaps by agreement of all or most members of the society. Establishment of a sovereign government from outside would be profitable if the anarchistic society could produce a surplus, an excess of output over subsistence needs, that could be extracted by the sovereign government and used to benefit those in control of the government. Establishment of a sovereign government from within would be profitable if a surplus could be extracted and used to benefit some group of residents of the society.

Given that a sovereign government exists and that the world contains others, each sovereign government must relate to other sovereign governments. It must defend itself and its constituents against invasion and harassment, and it must have agreements with other governments regarding trade, travel, communication, and other matters. Properly speaking, such relations are international affairs, and they are outside the scope of this book; nothing will be said about them. Nevertheless, the normative and positive conclusions of this book about domestic actions of governments have implications for international relations. At present, the only relevant conclusion is that conduct of relations with other sovereign governments is inherent in the notion of sovereignty.

In domestic matters, a sovereign government must make laws that provide for basic economic institutions, such as manufacturing corporations and banks, and it must provide for economic transactions and agreements. It must define and protect whatever personal and property rights are to exist The term *property rights* is sometimes used to include the right to control one's person and the results of one's productive efforts. Whether that term or some other is used, laws are needed that define and enforce the rights of workers. All these types of laws are needed, whether they provide for private property and production or not. If the economic system is to include private property and production, laws must provide legal instruments and rules for ownership and exchange of private property.

It is obvious to the most casual newspaper reader that the extent to which governments make laws and act in the interests of their citizens varies from one country to another. The basic theory of democracy is that it induces governments to further citizens' interests by providing citizens an orderly mechanism for turning rulers out of office if they fail to do so. It is obvious that this elective process works imperfectly, even in the best functioning democracies. The point of this book is that governments in most democratic governments fail badly to further the best interests of citizens. Pursuit of this point entails two important steps. The first, pursued in Chapters 3 through 8, consists in asking what governments should do in order to pursue citizens' interests and in comparing what they should do with what they do. The second step, pursued in Chapter 9, is to ask why the disparity between what governments do and what they should do is so great, even in democracies.

This chapter and the following are written entirely within the context of modern welfare economics: what should governments do to further the social efficiency and equity of an economy. The assumption that governments seek to improve the efficiency and equity of an economy is meant not to describe reality but to provide a set of justified government actions that can be compared with actions governments are observed to take.

A final comment about sovereign governments: The right to coerce its citizens is inherent in the notion of a sovereign government. It is not possible to understand what governments do and why they do it without understanding the concept of coercion. But *coercion* is an emotional word, and it is important to be clear about it.

The basic idea behind the word *coercion* is that people force others to engage in transactions against their will. The actual or threatened use of force is crucial. The fact that A restricts B's options to a set among which B would not have chosen had A not intervened is not enough to justify saying that A coerced B. In order to justify use of the word *coercion, A* must use or threaten to use whatever force is necessary to induce B to choose from among the transactions that are in A's interest.

Consider two examples. Suppose A hires B's workers away by paying them more than B did. Then A has restricted B's options, but A has not coerced B. Suppose, instead, that A threatens to kill B unless B releases workers so they can work for A. Then A has coerced B. The outcome may be almost the same in the two examples, but the means are entirely different. In some examples, the distinction may be fine, depending on how much force is used or threatened. But the basic distinction is crucial.[1]

In the United States, private coercion is made illegal by basic criminal and civil statutes.[2] After the preceding discussion, it should not be controversial to say that governments inevitably coerce their subjects. In the United States, governments make some decisions by two-thirds majority votes, some by majorities, and some by, or at the behest of, tiny minorities. In most countries, government decisions are normally made at the behest of tiny minorities. Only if every government decision had unanimous support among subjects could government avoid coercion. Whatever group opposes a government action must nevertheless abide by it. If government decides to increase taxes to pay for more atomic bombs, for more foreign aid, or for larger transfers to the poor, citizens must pay the higher taxes whether they favor the expenditure or not. Likewise, landlords risk fines or jail if they charge rents above the legal maximum for their New York apartments, regardless of whether they approve of rent control.

Philosophers and others have debated for centuries the extent to which it is legitimate for one group, say a majority, to coerce another group through government action. The contention here is that light can be shed on this issue by distinguishing between social efficiency and equity issues. Regarding social efficiency issues, it is deeply paradoxical to claim that one group should coerce another through government actions intended to improve the well-being of some members of one or both groups and to harm the well-being of no one—that is, to promote social efficiency.[3] Because government intervention to promote equity entails (again by definition) improvements in the well-being of some people at the expense of the well-being of others, there is a presumption that equity intervention requires coercion.

GOVERNMENT ACTIONS
TO ENSURE SOCIAL EFFICIENCY

The purpose here is to discuss what governments should do to ensure social efficiency of the economic system. The following list contains (with relatively minor exceptions to be discussed shortly) a sufficient set of government actions to ensure that the economy is socially efficient:

1. The government should relate to other sovereign governments in a variety of ways, including protection of its citizens and property from foreign seizure and harassment.
2. Government should define private property rights and provide the legal basis for private economic institutions, instruments for ownership, and exchange of services and property. Government should also establish police and court systems that protect rights of people to their persons, human capital, and material property.
3. Government must provide for and control the money supply and must levy taxes to finance the activities listed here.

This appears to be a short and simple list of actions governments should undertake. Certainly, it is a much smaller set of activities than governments undertake in any country. But complex and subtle issues are involved.

Determination of what set of laws is optimum to define property rights, provide for basic economic institutions, and facilitate economic transactions are issues for lawyers, not economists. It is certain that existing laws are much more complex than necessary, many having been passed to assist one group or another to gain special economic advantage.[4] Although these are legal issues, some special comments are needed on the concept of *property rights*. It is now common for economists to include human capital—one's accumulated education, training, and skills that have economic value—in that term. Thus providing for and protecting human capital means both permitting people to accumulate human capital as their self-interest dictates and permitting them to sell their services as they wish and for prices others will pay without coercion.

Property rights also include rights to own and exchange land and other natural resources, as well as man-made property. In recent years, scholarly papers on property rights have begun to discuss new interpretations of the term. For example, consider environmental protection. In the absence of legislation or common law to control polluting discharges, it is natural to say that people have a property right to pollute the environment unhampered. Laws intended to protect environmental quality invariably impose controls on polluting discharges and impose most costs of discharge abatement on owners of discharging facilities. This is usually referred to as the *polluter-pays principle*. Such laws can be said to confiscate polluters' property rights and to assign to users of the environment property rights to a clean environment. Such laws always provide partial or limited property rights to a clean environment and most do not permit their sale or transfer.

The point of this discussion is that the statement that governments must define and protect property rights is only partly clear. There are many kinds of property and many rights that may be defined and assigned to someone for each kind of property. As the environmental example shows, the absence of legislation assigning property rights is itself an implicit assignment of property rights. For our purposes here, property rights will be taken to be a clear-cut notion. Such rights can be thought of as providing for ownership and exchange of normal kinds of property. Some special property-rights problems are discussed later in this chapter.

In Chapter 1, the basic theorem of welfare economics was presented: Provided that technology permits competitive markets to exist and to value aspects of production and consumption that affect people's well-being, private markets will be competitive and socially efficient. Provided that technology satisfies the stated conditions, the set of government actions listed earlier in this chapter is known to be sufficient to ensure that private interest generates markets that are competitive and socially efficient. This set of government actions provides a legal framework for private economic institutions and markets, and provides for the security of investment in human and physical property, and provides that owners can use their human and physical capital in the most advantageous ways and retain most of the returns that markets permit them to make.[5] If technology permits competitive markets to exist, self-interest generates them. If any markets for inputs or outputs are monopolistic or otherwise imperfectly competitive, the desire for high returns to human and physical capital induces entry that makes them competitive. Likewise, if technology permits competitive markets to value important characteristics of production and consumption, the desire for high returns makes it profitable for participants in competitive markets to place appropriate values on all such characteristics. Economists have also long known that competitive markets are socially efficient if technology permits them to be. The usual restriction imposed by economists is that technology permits competitive markets to value important characteristics of production and consumption. Contrary conditions are frequently referred to as externalities.

The results just stated come as a great surprise to many people but are hardly controversial among economists. No subject has been studied more carefully or rigorously by economists. Dispute among economists about the social efficiency of private markets centers on the assumption that technology permits competitive markets to exist and to value aspects of production and consumption that affect people's well-being. Most economists believe that some or all of the following technological characteristics are important and prevent private markets from being socially efficient: increasing returns to scale, externalities, public goods and transactions and information costs. The contention here is that economists have underestimated the conditions in which technology permits private markets to be socially efficient.

The contention is that the set of three government actions listed earlier is sufficient to enable private markets to be socially efficient, almost without restrictions on technology. This contention ascribes much greater social value to private markets than most economists are accustomed to. Thus the argument must be developed and illustrated with care. I start here with a stark proof precisely on the abstract terms on which welfare economic analysis is conducted and then go on to illustrate and develop the analysis.

Suppose that government has carried out the three actions, but place no restrictions on technology except that production functions are well defined and limits have been imposed on production such that more output can be produced only by using more inputs.

Suppose the economy starts at some configuration P. *Configuration* means a description of the ways all inputs are used and outputs produced, the division of people's time between work and leisure, and the ways outputs are allocated among consumers. P has been reached by a set of private production and exchange activities. Either P is on the utility frontier or it is not. If it is, the economy is socially efficient, and there is nothing more for government to do. If it is not on the utility frontier, there must exist a set of reallocations of inputs and outputs that can make some people better off and none worse off. That is the meaning of being off the utility frontier. Call the configuration after such reallocations Q. Q is closer to the utility frontier than P. Then those who are made better off by the reallocations from P to Q have incentive to undertake the reallocations. Because no one is made worse off by the reallocations, no one has incentive to oppose them. Governments need play no role in moving the economy from P to Q.

Because the argument that private transactions can move the economy from P to Q applies to any configuration P such that P is off the utility frontier and Q is closer to it than P, it follows that private transactions will get the economy to the utility frontier—that is, will be socially efficient. When no confusion is likely, this result will be referred to as the theorem on the social efficiency of private markets. When it is necessary to distinguish this result from the theorem referred to earlier by the same name, they will be referred to respectively as the expanded and narrow theorems on social efficiency of private markets. The proof just presented is essentially that typically used in welfare economic analysis to establish the social efficiency of competitive markets. What distinguishes the expanded from the narrow theory is that the former makes no assumption about technology or other conditions that might result in competitive markets. In what follows, the term *government intervention* refers to actions of government other than the three listed earlier. Governments that restrict themselves to these three functions will be said to be noninterventionist.

The argument has been stated in stark, simple logic to make it transparent. To make it persuasive, considerable interpretation and illustration are required, and these activities occupy the remainder of this chapter and much of the remainder of this book.

When academic economists hear this argument, their invariable comment is "Yes, but how would the private sector deal with X?" X is always some issue that governments have tried to deal with and that economists have mostly assumed the private sector cannot deal with. Some good examples are public goods, nonexistent markets, transaction costs, externalities, and natural monopolies. Here, some general comments are made about the expanded theory, followed by discussion of specific issues.

The first observation is that the expanded theorem on social efficiency of private markets does not state that private markets can solve particular problems. Many so-called problems have no solutions, whether governments intervene or not. Thus the question posed in the previous paragraph is not quite appropriate. Sometimes those who ask the question make the implicit assumption that governments can solve the problem. That assumption needs to be defended at least as much as the contention that private markets can do the job.

The basic point of the expanded theorem on social efficiency of private markets is that private agreements can bring to bear any mechanism that governments can to get the economy to the utility frontier. If governments carry out the three basic activities listed in this chapter, no additional activity that is valuable in getting to the utility frontier is available to government that is not available in the same way to private parties. Private organizations can buy and hire inputs and produce and sell outputs. They can also undertake research and development, do market research, hold elections, conduct public opinion polls, spread risks, and so forth. Any form of voluntary organization or production that is available to government is available to private parties at the same costs and using the same technology of production, market and other research, and distribution.

The one thing that governments can do that private parties cannot do is to coerce people to take part in transactions that make them worse off. It will be argued subsequently that that capability is an important component of the appearance that government can solve many problems that private organizations cannot solve. At present, the point to be made is that coercion need play no part in moving the economy to the utility frontier. Starting anywhere off the utility frontier, there must exist a move to the frontier that the move's beneficiaries want to make voluntarily and that no one opposes because no one is made worse off.

Because they are accustomed to analyzing only a narrow class of private actions, such as production and exchange at fixed prices set by markets, some economists underestimate the ability of private activities to attain social efficiency. Yet they attribute to government broader horizons and more flexible modes of behavior. But unless governments intervene to prevent it artificially, private parties can employ—with the same technology, the same costs, and the same beneficial outputs— any mode of voluntary decision making, cooperative behavior, surveys of needs and tastes, production, and distribution that government can employ.

COMMENTS ON SPECIFIC ISSUES
ABOUT TECHNOLOGY

It was stated earlier that economists mostly agree that private markets can attain social efficiency provided technology enables competitive markets to exist and to place prices on aspects of production and consumption that affect people's well-being. The point made was that the conditions economists think to be important for this purpose are sufficient but not necessary. It was shown that private agreements can attain social efficiency without government intervention because only voluntary actions are needed and private markets have access to all the same voluntary procedures as governments.

Most economists accept this simple logic. But many do not accept its logical implication that government intervention can contribute nothing to attainment of social efficiency. Here the case will be made more persuasive by discussing several specific characteristics widely believed by economists to justify government intervention.[6]

Transaction Costs and Nonexistent Markets

A frequent contention is that high transaction costs prevent certain markets from existing and thus from valuing some activities with prices that represent benefits and costs of the activities.[7] The inference is that government should intervene to provide at least approximately the resource allocation that would be provided by the nonexistent market.

Transaction costs refers to costs of organizing a transaction in contrast with the cost of the commodity when it is bought and sold. For example, it may be costly to find a buyer for your home or firm or to find just the home or firm you would like to buy. Such search costs are transaction costs. In recent years, much attention has been paid by economists to transaction costs entailed by the need to acquire information about technology and markets. Like other transaction costs, information costs are logically independent of the scale of the intended transaction. Thus they give rise to increasing returns: The information cost per unit produced or marketed falls as the number of units produced or marketed increases, which allows the fixed information costs to be spread over more units produced or marketed.[8] There can be no doubt that transaction costs can be large and that they prevent some markets from existing. Because of the cost of ascertaining relevant risks and of placing people and property in appropriate risk categories, many contingencies cannot be insured against. For example, you cannot typically buy insurance against the contingency that your skills will be made obsolete by new technology or against the contingency that your plant will be confiscated by government if you invest in a foreign country. Transaction costs are real resource costs. Markets are worth forming and voluntary agreements form them if benefits exceed costs of doing so. Benefits are improvements in well-being that result from the commodities traded; costs are production and transaction costs associated with the market activity. If private parties do not form the markets, it is because benefits do not exceed costs of doing so. Government intervention is justified only if government has access to technology of market formation that is not available to private parties. But the fact of government intervention does not eliminate or reduce transaction costs. No one has ever indicated why government might be able to incur lower transaction costs than private parties. Sometimes economists claim that private markets generate insufficient information relevant to social efficiency because information is a "public good" and private markets cannot produce public goods efficiently.

Public Goods

Much of the contemporary argument for government intervention focuses on public goods. *Public goods* is a terrible term. Most of the discussion in the economics literature refers to services, not commodities, and the word *public* immediately suggests that governments should or must provide them. To make matters worse, the term is not used consistently or precisely. Although the term has a technical meaning, many economists use it to refer to almost any service provided by government.

To provide justification for government intervention or provision, instead of a mere description of the fact, *public goods* must be given its technical meaning. A public good is a commodity (including services) whose consumption by additional people requires no additional resources.[9] Resources are necessary for the production of public goods, and more resources are required to produce them at high quality; but it takes no more resources to enable more people to consume the commodity. Frequently, a second characteristic—nonexcludability—is added to the definition. A commodity is nonexcludable if, once it has been produced, consumption by additional people is impossible or expensive to prevent.

Many examples of public goods are given in the economics literature. National security, valuable new knowledge produced by research and development, a clean environment, radio and TV spectra, streetlights, and lighthouses are probably the most important. For example, national governments produce national security by devoting resources to military forces that can prevent invasion by foreign forces. More resources appropriately employed provide more security, so the quality of the service can be improved by use of additional resources. Yet it costs no more to provide a given amount of national security to the 50 states than to 49 states, excluding New Jersey; and it costs no more to protect the 50 states if their population is 240 million than if it is 230 million. Finally, protection cannot be withheld, at least not easily, from particular groups of people, say those whose family names begin with Z. Thus national security satisfies both criteria of a public good.

Research and development generate new knowledge that can be used to produce new and improved products. Additional resources devoted to research generate additional new knowledge. Once produced, the new knowledge can be used by additional people without reducing its availability to other users. Potential users can be excluded from use of new knowledge (by patents and secrecy, for example), but exclusion is temporary, imperfect, and expensive.

A clean environment is valuable to people for health, aesthetic, and recreational reasons. Natural processes and—much more so—production and consumption activities pollute the environment. Resources can be devoted to cleaning the environment and to abatement of its pollution (as by treating wastes before discharge to the environment). More resources used for that purpose make the environment cleaner. It costs no more if a few extra people enjoy a clean environment, to the extent that their use is not polluting. Finally, it is difficult or impossible to exclude people from the benefits of a clean environment. These statements apply most strongly to ambient air. At least ambient air satisfies both definitional criteria of a public good.

TV and radio spectra are public goods in that, once produced, programs can be watched or heard by additional people at no additional cost to producers or to other consumers. But modern technology provides means of exclusion at modest cost.

Lighthouses are minor but pure examples of public goods that satisfy both definitional criteria.[10] Streetlights are similar, but roads are not. To the extent that roads are crowded, additional users impose costs on other users. To the extent that they are used by motor vehicles, exclusion is cheap and easy by means of licenses and fuel taxes.

Why are public goods thought to justify government intervention? Three arguments are given in the literature. First, if use by additional people requires no additional resources, social efficiency requires that users not be deterred by charges. Anyone who can benefit must be free to consume the public good at no cost. Otherwise some people could benefit by increased consumption of the public good without making anyone worse off. Thus if a service satisfies the first definitional criterion of a public good—zero extra costs of adding a consumer—then it is socially inefficient to exclude anyone for whom the marginal utility of its consumption is positive, even if exclusion is technically possible. Second, if the public good is nonexcludable, people are assumed to be motivated to refuse to pay for its use. Each person is assumed to reason that, if produced, the public good will be available to consume whether the user pays or not. Especially if the affected group is large, each person may reason that one individual's refusal to agree to pay is unlikely to prevent the public good from being produced. This is referred to as the free-rider problem. Third, if people are asked what the public good is worth to them by someone trying to decide whether to produce it, they may believe (perhaps correctly) that their answers will influence what they will be asked to pay for production of the good. It is thought that this motivates people to understate their preferences for public goods. All three of these factors make it difficult for private parties to produce public goods in ways that reimburse the producer for production costs and permit socially efficient use.

A characteristic of the entire public goods literature is an almost automatic belief that these three issues justify government intervention. In fact, they are simply characteristics of public goods, and there is no analysis or evidence in the literature that governments can produce them with greater social efficiency than private parties.

Suppose that government proposes to produce a public good and finance it by taxes levied on its beneficiaries. It puts the proposal to a vote among the intended beneficiaries of the public good. Suppose that production of the public good is desirable and that the proposal will improve the well-being of all those affected. Then the vote will be unanimous. But a private party with access to the same information and technology can propose a contract to the same people, and with the same terms of payment as the government proposal. The contract can be written so it becomes effective only if all sign. All will sign because each is made better off by the contract's terms. Thus a private agreement can accomplish exactly what the government proposal can accomplish, and on the same terms.

The common response at this point is "How can a private group acquire the information about benefits, given the incentive for consumers to understate benefits?" The answer is that it can employ the same techniques of market research that government can, and on the same terms. No one knows how to induce complete demand revelation for public goods, but the problem applies as much to government as to private parties.

Another common response is "How do you know people will not refuse to sign the private contract, believing they can hold out for better terms?" Again, the same argument applies to the government proposal and to ensuing votes. Strategic voting is an inherent part of public-good decision making and is neither more nor less important with government or private decision making.[11]

The point here is a special case of the point made earlier. The same techniques of production, market research, financing, or decision making available to governments in solving public goods problems are available to private parties on the same terms. All are likely to be imperfect compared with economists' ideal for resource allocation.

The important issue with public goods is excludability. If consumption can be prevented cheaply (that is, with modest transaction costs), then private producers can recover production costs from consumers of that public good. For a pure public good, fixed charges similar to membership fees can be levied on consumers. Then that public good is not produced unless total consumer benefits exceed production costs. Furthermore, competition among actual and potential producers can ensure that charges are as low as possible, consistent with cost recovery. Private financing has the defect that it excludes some potential consumers for whom the public good's marginal utility is positive but less than the fixed charge. That problem can be obviated if the private producer can effectively discriminate among consumers; low prices can be charged to consumers to whom consumption of the public good has little value. Government production has similar problems. The public good must be paid for, and any method of financing that government might use entails distortions. Financing from general tax revenues is probably among the worst ways to provide most public goods. Distortions from taxes may be large, and general revenue financing removes the assurance that production takes place only if benefits exceed costs. The conclusion is that, if government has any means to estimate benefits and compare them with costs, the same method can be used both to decide to produce and to finance production of the public good by private parties.

Public goods certainly cause resource allocation problems, whether they are produced by government or by private groups. Government intervention is justified only if exclusion is expensive or impossible and if there is a mechanism not only to compare benefits with costs but also to restrict production to situations in which benefits exceed costs. Fortunately, as we shall see, public goods that satisfy these stringent requirements are much less important than one would infer from the attention paid to them in the economics literature.

National security along with most basic elements of foreign policy are certainly important examples of public goods. But their provision by national governments is intrinsic to the notion of sovereignty, and excludability is too difficult. They cannot be provided by the private sector.

Valuable new knowledge resulting from use of resources for research and development is also an important example of a public good. Much technical progress and economic growth result from research and development. Basic research, much more than applied research and development, has the characteristics of a public good; and beneficiaries of basic research are almost impossible to identify or exclude. Basic research cannot be financed adequately by groups that intend to recover costs from beneficiaries. Whether government can do a better job of resource allocation to basic research than can the private sector is unknown. It depends on the incentive systems in government and in such private institutions as universities and foundations. Fortunately, basic research is not costly. In the United States, only about 0.3 percent of GNP is devoted to basic research. About 65 percent of basic research is funded by the national government, and the remainder is funded by industry, universities, foundations, and other private institutions. Applied research and development are more closely related to new products and productive processes than is basic research, so funding by groups who recover costs by selling resulting products to beneficiaries is more feasible. How feasible depends on how carefully property rights in the new knowledge are defined and protected by patents, copyrights, and related legal devices. About 45 percent of applied research is funded by the national government, but this is mostly for activities (especially those related to national security) in which the national government will be the important user of any resulting new technology. Most of the remainder is funded by private corporations.[12] Most information production that is germane to transaction costs is in the nature of very applied research and can be financed from sales that are facilitated by the information. There is no reason or evidence in the economics literature that suggests that governments can generate information that is relevant to detailed transactions with greater social efficiency than can private markets.

A clean environment is also a valuable public good. Some environmental problems are global, and solving them is beyond the capability of both private groups and individual national governments. Many environmental problems are localized, pertaining to a particular stream, lake, or tract of real estate. In such cases, private groups often have the capability to exclude, and hence to recover environmental protection costs from, beneficiaries and can finance pollution abatement as efficiently as governments. In other cases, private groups could provide efficient resource allocation if governments provided better definitions of property rights—to water in a stream, for example. Many environmental problems pervade a metropolitan area or waterway system, and private groups probably cannot exclude, and hence cannot recover, significant amounts of environmental protection costs from beneficiaries. A proposed government solution in such cases is discussed shortly.

Modern technology has provided inexpensive means of excluding people from TV and, less easily, radio programs. Cable TV, scrambling, and cassettes are common exclusionary devices for TV that permit private groups to exclude and hence to recover program costs from beneficiaries and to finance production as efficiently as government. Furthermore, technology has removed earlier limitations on the number of available channels, thus permitting competitive production. Once again, a variety of contractual schemes is available to optimize consumption in almost any circumstances. Governments in nearly all countries produce or regulate radio and TV programs, but their main goal is undoubtedly control over content, not efficient resource allocation.

Natural and Other Monopolies

Prevention or control of monopolies is a justification for government intervention often found in the economics literature. Government activities that fall under this heading include antimonopoly laws, government ownership or regulation of public utilities, and government regulation of many other industries.

Scale economies means that, at fixed input prices, unit costs fall as output increases within a center of production.[13] At sufficiently small outputs, scale economies are present in all production activities, including not only manufacturing but also services and agriculture. In all activities, scale economies are exhausted at some sufficiently large output, meaning that unit costs level off and may rise as output increases. Scale economies cause resource allocation problems only if unit costs continue to fall up to or near output levels that equal market demand at prices near unit costs. In that case, cost is lowest if the market's entire output is produced by a single production unit, and the production unit is said to be a natural monopoly.

Government intervention is thought to be justified because firm owners maximize their profit and well-being by charging a price that is above average and marginal cost. The narrow theorem on social efficiency of private markets shows that the result is production of too little of the commodity. It would be possible to produce more and sell it on terms that would make customers better off and owners no worse off.[14]

Economists are concerned about natural monopolies because they assume that the only alternatives are an unconstrained profit-maximizing firm or one that is owned or regulated by government. In fact, many other possibilities can be imagined. Potential customers can organize a firm or cooperative and finance it by a two-part tariff. A profit-making firm can propose to produce the product and finance it with a similar two-part tariff, undertaking investment only after enough customers have signed up to justify proposed outlays. An organization of customers could take bids for construction of a needed plant and/or from companies proposing to operate the plant. Once a socially efficient proposal has been made, it will command unanimous approval of customers.

Depending on the nature of the products, the transaction costs of identifying customers and obtaining agreement may be large or small. The most important contemporary examples of natural monopolies are local systems in which distribution must take place through fixed channels. Examples are natural gas, electricity, water, and liquid wastes. Mostly, natural monopolies are confined to distribution systems, which can be owned separately from production facilities. In all such cases, most customers are such people as owners of local residences and commercial establishments, who are a well-defined group and are easy to identify. Thus transaction costs of identifying customers are small. In addition, excludability is easy with such products, so there is typically no public-goods aspect of significant natural monopolies.

Loss of social efficiency from natural or other monopolies can be avoided by flexibility. If customers are not satisfied with one arrangement, they can try another. If one firm makes excessive profits, others can enter and bid them away, restoring social efficiency.[15] When governments intervene to regulate or own firms, they invariably prevent entry and competition by other firms. The result is that such firms become stronger and longer-lasting monopolists than they need be.

Almost all monopolies, natural or otherwise, that persist and do great harm are able to do so because governments prevent entry. Public utility regulation, licensing, and import controls are common ways that governments sustain monopolies.

BENEFIT-COST ANALYSIS

An important point to remember is that resource allocation problems do not arise with public goods because additional customers can be accommodated at little or no cost. Private ownership, production, and pricing arrangements can be found to match or better the social efficiency of resource allocation under government production or subsidy. Competition or cooperative arrangements can ensure consumption at minimum cost. All participation is voluntary. The important problem with public goods is that the high transaction cost or the impossibility of exclusion may make it difficult to identify beneficiaries, to measure benefits, and to collect revenues needed to cover production costs. As has been seen, people are motivated to understate benefits of public goods to them if they cannot be excluded from consumption. Fortunately, this fact means that only a small set of commodities satisfies the criterion and causes problems with resource allocation.

Difficulty of excluding nonpaying consumers is as much a problem for government as for private provision of public goods. Whatever technology of exclusion is available to government is available to private parties on the same terms.

Governments have sometimes employed a device intended to achieve an approximation to social efficiency in this situation, and economists have written about it extensively.[16] This device, benefit-cost analysis, is especially valuable for governments.

To make the case for benefit-cost analysis as strong as possible, consider an example of what is perhaps its best application, environmental protection.[17] Consider a metropolitan area whose air is badly polluted by discharges from factories, homes, vehicles, government buildings, and the like. Because there are thousands of discharge sources and millions of people affected, there is no way that a private agreement can exclude people from the benefits of a voluntary abatement program. Furthermore, benefits of abatement vary greatly among residents and visitors in the metropolitan area depending on where they live and work, their health, and how they value improvements in air quality. Knowing they cannot be excluded, people are not willing to pay their share of abatement costs or to reveal their valuations of abatement. Indeed, they lack incentive to study or think hard about the value of cleaner air to them.

A possible solution to the problem is for government to estimate schedules showing benefits and costs of various air qualities and related discharge volumes. Having estimated the schedules, welfare economics says that the optimum air quality is that which equates marginal benefits and marginal costs.[18] Government then passes laws to induce dischargers to abate discharges to the volume associated with the optimum air quality. Each discharger should be permitted the discharge to the volume that equates its marginal abatement cost to that of all others and to the marginal benefit of abatement.

The cost schedule can be estimated, perhaps with considerable difficulty, by ascertaining the least-cost set of changes associated with each discharge volume. Possible changes include switches to clean fuels, smaller cars, movement of polluting industries elsewhere, scrubbers on smokestacks, and so forth.

Estimating the benefit schedule is the key to the analysis because direct inquiries or market research cannot be used. In principle, the benefit of a given air quality is the sum of the valuations that people place on that air quality. Some of the benefits may be reduced deterioration rates of materials, and they can be ascertained by laboratory experiments. Improved health is likely to be the largest benefit of air pollution abatement. Likely reductions in medical expenditures can be inferred from studies of medical spending in relation to income, health status, and other variables. The most difficult and controversial part of the analysis is estimating the subjective value people place on avoidance of health risks. As a practical matter, estimation of the relationship between air quality and health is likely to be the most uncertain part of the analysis.

Although the foregoing procedure achieves resource allocation on the utility frontier, it cannot reach a point on the frontier that makes no one worse off than before the abatement program. Usually, owners of discharge sources are required to pay most abatement costs, and general government tax revenues are used to subsidize remaining costs. Governments never try to identify beneficiaries and require them to pay pollution abatement costs. This procedure entails an imputation of property rights in clean air to users of the air. It is inconceivable that discharge source ownership would be so precisely related to abatement benefits that no one is made worse off by the abatement program.

By and large, those who benefit most from abatement favor the program, and those forced to pay large abatement costs oppose it. In many situations, including many proposals for which total benefits are less than total costs, the former group outnumbers the latter group. Thus a political process dependent on majority voting may adopt the proposal for a government abatement program. But coercion of the minority is a crucial part of the procedure. Thus, in principle, government can undertake the program whereas private parties cannot.

For many of the public-goods production projects proposed by governments, benefit estimation is inherently difficult. There is probably no benefit estimation study in the United States that a large sample of good economists could agree is within 50 percent of the truth. To make matters worse, most government benefit-cost analyses are systematically distorted. Although benefit-cost analysis is undertaken by many national government agencies for many kinds of activities, it is remarkable that the results are almost never relied on by appointed and elected officials who actually make decisions in Washington.[19] In fact, they tend to be contemptuous of the technique. One reason may be that benefit-cost analyses carried out by or at the behest of government agencies bear almost no resemblance to the careful techniques presented in economics textbooks.[20] As is explained in Chapter 9, government agencies always want to justify their expansion. Careful benefit-cost analysis would cast doubt on the social justification of most activities of most government agencies.[21] Thus most benefit-cost calculations are little more than accounting exercises intended to make the case for larger budgets and more authority for the agency involved.

The most dramatic example of this is the national government's environmental protection program. Ironically, environmental protection is by far the most natural application of benefit-cost analysis. The attitude of strong environmentalists in Congress has been that the American people don't want to hear about costs, they want clean air. Congress has written into law discharge standards that are not based on any benefit-cost calculations, and it has written into law criteria for choosing standards that are inconsistent with use of benefit-cost analysis.[22]

In fact, most government interventions have little to do with social efficiency. It will be shown in Chapter 9 that, based on the positive theory of government, stories similar to that of the environmental protection program are exactly what should be expected.

A summary judgment regarding benefit-cost analysis is that, if done as carefully as possible, it probably provides a rough guide to justifiable government interference in a few areas, especially that of environmental protection. Potentially, it may be able to provide a rough guide to improvements in one or two other public-good resource allocation problems, notably government research and development programs. In any case in which benefit-cost analysis is used, judgment is needed that the positive net benefit to citizens as a whole justifies the negative net benefits that inevitably accrue to those harmed by such government programs as environmental protection.

In practice, it would be difficult to obtain a consensus among informed economists that government intervention has done more good than harm in the two most natural subjects for benefit-cost analysis: environmental protection and production of new knowledge by research and development.

APPENDIX:
INCENTIVES AND
GOVERNMENT INTERVENTION

The main point of this chapter has been that private groups can engage in any voluntary means of production or decision making on the same terms that government can. Individuals are motivated to take actions that improve their well-being, and the set of such actions places the economy on the utility frontier without government intervention.

The argument can be summarized by the statement that private incentives are sufficient to get the economy to the utility frontier without government intervention. But are they necessary? It has been argued that government has no mechanism needed to get the economy to the utility frontier that is not also available to the private sector. The reverse may also be true. The private sector may have no mechanism needed to get the economy to the utility frontier that is not also available to government. If so, it may not matter much to what extent government intervenes. The most cursory glance at the damage governments do and have done around the world to economic efficiency shows that it matters greatly how governments intervene.

The question asked here is whether there is some way for government to intervene that can also get the economy to the utility frontier. This issue is not only important; it is also difficult. There is only one way for governments to avoid intervention, but there are limitless ways to intervene. What class of interventions is to be studied? The question is also difficult for a more subtle reason, which is discussed here, in the context of welfare economics.

The actual incentives of government as to amount and form of intervention are discussed in Chapter 9. Here, the aim is to ask whether there is any conceivable intervention (aside from the one or two exceptional examples discussed at the end of the chapter) that could get the economy to the utility frontier. To make the question worth discussing, it is necessary to assume that government is motivated to get the economy to the utility frontier.

The question is how far to push the assumption. Consider an extreme example. Suppose, as many nineteenth- and twentieth-century utopians have, that the mere fact of working for government, or at least for a certain type of government, induces people to pursue social efficiency instead of private gain. Then all that would be necessary would be to establish the right kind of government and have it own all property and production facilities, and the problem would be solved.

Most people and nearly all economists regard as absurd the notion that people can be made into saints by working for a particular form of government. But the example makes clear that some assumptions are necessary as to who in government is motivated to achieve social welfare and who must be given more prosaic incentives.

Consider another extreme example—a "command" economy in which the national government owns everything. There is a central planning board, assumed to be motivated to achieve social efficiency. There are also many government-owned production facilities run by people with ordinary human motives. The economy operates by the central planning board calculating optimum inputs and outputs for each production facility and optimum quantities of each commodity for each citizen to consume. The planning board simply tells each plant manager what inputs to use to produce what outputs and where to send the outputs. Managers are assumed to obey the planning board's instruction, perhaps because they will be punished if they do not. This is a distant approximation to the way most Marxian socialist economies work. In a pre–World War II debate about the viability of socialism, critics assumed that this is the only way a socialist economy could work. They rightly claimed that the system would place an impossible burden of data gathering and processing on the planning board. The critics lost the debate because socialist theorists showed that systems of intervention could be devised that placed much smaller burdens on the planning board.[23]

That debate led to the Lange-Lerner theory of socialist resource allocation. To this day, it is the only extant theory of pervasive government intervention that seems to have any hope of providing a set of incentives that might get the economy to the utility frontier. It is analyzed here in some detail.

Suppose government owns some set of production activities. In principle, it makes no difference whether the set consists of all facilities or of a subset, such as those that it is believed would not be sufficiently competitive under private ownership. A central planning board is assumed to be motivated to get the economy to the utility frontier. It tells the appointed manager of each production facility what products it can produce and the price at which they can be sold. The planning board also sets wages for each kind of labor. Facility managers know prices of inputs they buy and outputs they produce and sell. The planning board tells managers that they can buy and sell only at those prices but that they should buy input quantities and sell output quantities that maximize the facility's profit.[24] Likewise, workers can work where they wish at the wage set by the planning board. Any profits made by a production facility go to the planning board, and losses are made up by the board (disposition of profits is discussed shortly). The board must adjust prices and wages until they equate supply and demand for each product and kind of worker. It does that by choosing an initial price based on whatever evidence it has or can find about supply and demand conditions. If demand exceeds supply at that price, the board raises price. If supply exceeds demand, it lowers price. Similarly with wages. This is roughly the way competitive private markets seek equilibrium prices and quantities, and it is likely that the system would converge to the right prices and quantities if the planning board were sufficiently quick and flexible in changing wages and prices. It is likely that the resulting resource allocation would be a tolerable approximation to short-run social efficiency.

Why would the facility manager comply with the board's instruction to maximize profit? In a private company, the owner keeps the resulting profits and is thus motivated to make them as large as possible to maximize personal well-being. The socialist manager, however, cannot keep the profits.

There is of course separation between ownership and management in large contemporary private corporations, and some observers believe that managers pursue their own goals rather than those of the diffused shareholders of the corporation.[25] But that does not really matter. The possibility of entry implies that the corporation could not compete with other institutions (say with smaller corporations in which owners were managers) if the large corporation's prices were higher. Likewise, it could not compete for capital funds if shareholders could obtain higher returns elsewhere (say in smaller corporations). These statements are correct in the long run and in the absence of government intervention.

If it is assumed that the planning board knows each government-owned production unit's cost curve, representing least-cost production at each output, then the board could ascertain whether managers were producing as cheaply as possible. But that places an enormous burden of information gathering and processing on the board. The whole idea of this decentralized socialist model is that information peculiar to production units would be gathered and processed at that level. The conclusion is inescapable: Without the profit motive, and especially without the threat of being put out of business by more efficient competitors, socialist managers would lack incentive to pursue cost minimization and profit maximization except to the extent that the planning board could detect departures from those policies. Planning boards could detect only gross departures at best.

The situation is actually much worse. Suppose there is a production technique that can improve the product, produce a new product, or produce the old product more cheaply. Managers lack incentive to seek such innovations because they cannot keep any resulting profits. Innovations would have to come mainly from the central planning board, which again requires it to have detailed information not only about local conditions but also about alternative technologies.

An obvious compromise solution is to permit production units to retain a share, say half, of profits. In many actual private enterprise economies, that is about all owners are permitted to retain, after paying taxes. If the production unit is told to reinvest retained profits, then the planning board loses control over investment. More important, the workers and management, whose behavior determines cost and profits, do not benefit from the profits their efforts generate, and therefore the retained profits do not motivate them to efficient production. If workers and managers can keep retained profits for their own use, then the prospect motivates them to maximize profits. But then the planning board loses control over compensation of workers and managers. In a privately owned economy, profit (defined as the excess of revenue over competitive capital and other costs) is a temporary reward for unusually efficient production. Although substantial returns are sometimes made, they are bid away by entrants attracted by the high returns to be made. Whether that would happen in the socialist economy depends on investment policies of the planning board.

This raises the issue of investment funds. Investment decisions must be made by the planning board. Otherwise, industries will be gradually privatized. The board would have available for investment the excess of unretained profits over losses of the government-owned enterprises. It should also be permitted to borrow funds from the public. In principle, investment should be at the level that equates the rate of return to capital to the public's rate of time preference—that is, their preference for present over future consumption. Investment should not be financed by taxes or by increases in the money supply because the public cannot reflect its time preference if these devices are used.

How would the planning board allocate funds? Production unit managers would have to make proposals to the board for funds for unit expansion, modernization, and innovation for new products and processes. To evaluate such proposals, the planning board would need detailed local and technological information. Experience with nationalized business in many countries shows that managers of loss-making businesses can make superficially plausible proposals that they could turn losses into profits if they had money for modernization and that central planners have great difficulty evaluating such proposals. Similar problems would exist regarding establishment of new business units.

The claim that the planning board would make mistakes is neither here nor there. Investments—especially those involving product and process innovations—are inherently risky, and private entrepreneurs and investors make many mistakes. The issue is that people who do not stand to make gains from successful innovations and to suffer losses from unsuccessful innovations lack incentive to seek the best and most persuasive proposals, and evaluating proposals would require the planning board to have enormous amounts of local and specific information. The planning board could always show a return to investments in excess of interest costs by underinvesting in innovative activities and by permitting production units to charge monopoly prices. But neither tactic would generate socially efficient resource allocation.

The two major incentive issues in nationalized business are at the level of minimizing costs at the production-unit level and in allocating investment funds. In both areas, the motive for private gain that private organizations have is removed by government ownership. In each case, it is necessary to assume that detailed information on local conditions is in some way available to a central planning board that is motivated to achieve socially efficient production. How they would obtain and process such information is a mystery. Equally important, it is necessary to assume that the planning board is composed of utterly moral people, determined to pursue social efficiency by intelligent investment of other people's money even though they have no stake in socially efficient allocations of funds they invest.

Thus, under the conceptual model of decentralized socialist production, incentive problems arise both at the production unit and at the planning board levels. At both levels, problems are caused by the fact that those who must make decisions have no personal stake in socially efficient outcomes.

FOUR

Governments
and Equity

The discussion of applied welfare economics, which in Chapter 3 was concerned with government actions to promote social efficiency, continues here, but with the focus on government actions to promote equity. I continue to assume that government is motivated to improve the functioning of the economy.

As was pointed out in Chapter 1, equity is concerned with the fairness of the distribution of well-being. Whereas Chapter 3 was concerned with actions to place the economy on the utility frontier, the concern is now with government actions to choose among points on, or at least near, the utility frontier.

The first question to ask is whether welfare economics can have anything to say about equity issues. It is not difficult to imagine that everyone prefers that governments undertake actions that make some groups better off without making others worse off. As has been shown, such government actions can command unanimous consent. But if people typically prefer more of at least some commodities and less of none (which is true if commodity prices are positive and consumers can spend their limited funds as they please) then it seems unlikely that there can be consensus about government actions to alter the distribution of well-being. That, indeed, is a key issue. It suggests that government programs to alter the distribution of well-being cannot command unanimity and instead require coercion of people made worse off by the altered distribution. One implication is that a criterion other than unanimity is required for equity choices. A second implication is that only governments can engage in redistribution because private groups cannot legally coerce members of society. These are thorny issues.

Other issues also merit discussion. Most people presume that there is a cost to government attempts to redistribute well-being. Starting from the utility frontier, there must be a cost in the sense of a reduction in the well-being of one group if well-being of another is to be improved by government programs. More than that, there is a presumption that government attempts to redistribute well-being result in a reduction in the average level of well-being—that is, in a movement away from the utility frontier. If so, it is important to ask how the cost varies with the amount of redistribution. Finally, the reduction in both the average well-being and that of particular groups is likely to depend on the mechanism by which redistribution is carried out.

Economists are accustomed to discussing equity issues in terms of distribution of income. All economists understand that income is not the only determinant of economic well-being. Most obviously, one's well-being depends not only on one's income but also on prices of commodities one buys. Prices vary somewhat from one place to another but, in the United States and most countries, much more from one time to another. Price indices can be used to convert money income into real income (a much better measure of purchasing power), but price movements may affect the distribution of well-being among generations and among stages in the life cycle. In addition, one's well-being depends not only on one's real income but also on how long and hard one has to work for it and on what work is done. Economists are driven to use of income as an approximate measure of well-being partly by lack of better measures. They have long known that reductions in hours worked have been an important component in increases in U.S. living standards during the twentieth century. But that source of improvement in well-being is not captured by income data. There has also been a reduction in the arduousness of work, as machinery has replaced human muscle. But that is even more difficult to measure. In an integrated and monetized economy such as the United States, income is a good approximation to well-being, at least if income is defined and measured carefully. Even so, it provides better comparisons across space than through time. In this chapter, income is being used freely as an index of well-being, but only few changes would be needed if a better measure were substituted.

COMPETITIVE INCOME DISTRIBUTION

The starting point for a discussion of equity issues must be the concept of a competitive income distribution. In Chapter 3, a set of government actions sufficient to generate a socially efficient resource allocation was prescribed. Suppose that governments undertake those activities but no others. Suppose that government revenues required to finance these activities are raised by taxes that have the least possible effect on private resource allocation.[1] Such a tax system can be referred to as socially efficient, even though it may not be equitable.

Then, as shown in Chapter 3, the private sector would engage in activities that put the economy on the utility frontier, that is, are socially efficient. This set of private activities generates a set of payments to input owners in which the owner of each input is paid the value of the input's marginal product in the activity (or activities) that makes its owner as well off as possible. Because all inputs are privately owned, the input payments generate an income to each input owner. The aggregate of such payments generates a distribution of income to all input owners.

Again from Chapter 3, the resulting set of production activities would not be entirely competitive in economists' traditional use of that term. Some activities would be sole producers of a product for a market (for example, natural monopolies, perhaps owned by consumers of the product), some would be producers of goods that are public in some degree, and some might be nonprofit institutions. All would produce as cheaply as possible and would therefore pay input owners the value of the marginal products of inputs used. In particular, capital input owners would be paid the value of the marginal product of their capital; there would be little profit beyond such amounts.[2]

The competitive distribution of income described briefly in Chapter 2 results entirely from competitive input and output markets. The income distribution characterized here results partly from competitive markets and partly from private market arrangements that resemble those under competition but may not satisfy all the usual characteristics of competition. Nevertheless, the resulting income distribution will be referred to as the *competitive income distribution*. Because it is the income distribution that results from a socially efficient resource allocation, a more logical term would be the *socially efficient income distribution*. But that term suggests ethical approval, so it is not used here.

The competitive income distribution depends mainly on the distribution of natural abilities and on the ownership distribution of physical and human capital. If a small group of people owned most of the physical capital in the economy, they would have much higher incomes than most people. Likewise, if a small group of people was much better educated or had much more productive skills than most people, then their incomes would be much higher than those of most people. Thus, in the long run, income distribution depends on natural abilities, on access to educational and training programs, on savings, and on inheritance patterns.

The countries with greatest income inequality in the world are mostly poor countries in which there is little physical or human capital.[3] In such countries, land is the predominant kind of capital, and if most of it is owned by a few people, great inequality results. In fact, this observation leads to the key to understanding the characteristic time path of income distribution in the course of economic development. The amount of land is approximately fixed, and once ownership becomes concentrated in a few hands, income distribution may remain very unequal for many decades. Man-made physical and human capital, in contrast, are produced by economic activity, and high returns to these kinds of capital motivate their production, lowering their returns.

Thus great inequality in income distributions because of inequality in ownership of human and man-made physical capital persists less long than inequality because of concentrated land ownership. Major exceptions are in countries in which governments prevent the normal competitive process of bidding down high returns to physical and human capital. It is not accidental that much of the world's worst domestic violence occurs in countries in which great inequality persists because of collusion between governments and owners of large amounts of land and other physical capital.

In the early stages of economic development, with annual income per capita no more than about $200, a few people are unusually well placed in terms of health, education, skills, and physical capital ownership to take advantage of growth opportunities as development begins. The result is that economic growth is accompanied by increasing income inequality. Using figures that approximate 1980 prices, after annual income per capita passes $1,000 or so, income inequality decreases with further growth. Both human and physical capital accumulate as a natural response to higher incomes and because the returns to both kinds of capital are high. Physical capital (which is more unequally owned than human capital in most societies) may accumulate more rapidly than human capital, and the share of physical capital in total income falls.[4] That shift in input shares reduces inequality. In addition, human capital becomes less unequal at high income levels. Although education is by no means the only dimension of human capital, it is the most important. At high average income levels, increasing proportions of the labor force have access to large amounts and high qualities of education, with the result that inequality of earned (that is nonproperty) income falls.[5] Thus the normal competitive process of increasing supplies of inputs whose returns are great has the consequence of reducing inequality in the personal income distribution during the course of economic development. There are important variants among countries, but the pattern is pervasive.

What is the competitive income distribution in the United States? Nobody knows, because the actual income distribution differs from it in a variety of ways, by far the most important being effects of taxes levied by governments and transfer payments by governments to various groups of people. Transfer payments discourage work and earnings, whereas high marginal income tax rates discourage both work and savings and capital accumulation. Nevertheless, economists have estimated the accounting effects of taxes and transfers. These estimates answer the question: What would the income distribution be in the absence of taxes and transfers if there were no effect of their removal on resource allocation? Even that question is difficult to answer.

The most careful study of this problem is summarized in Table 8. It shows the shares of total income received by each population quintile in the income distribution, from the poorest at the top of the table to the richest at the bottom. The second column shows income shares of the quintile groups before their taxes are subtracted and before transfers they received are added. The third column shows the quintile shares after all important federal, state, and local government taxes have been subtracted and all important government transfers added. The data are for 1970 but have probably not changed much since then. Complete equality would be represented by entries of 20 percent in each line of the relevant column.

The second column is an approximation to the U.S. competitive income distribution. It shows that income per capita in the highest income quintile is just over 2.25 times the average, whereas income per capita in the lowest is only about 25 percent of the average. The right column shows that government taxes and transfers had a substantial effect on the personal income distribution. In the after-tax-transfer distribution, the highest income quintile had per capita income about twice the average, whereas the lowest income quintile had per capita income equal to about 40 percent of the average. Taxes and transfers raised the income share of the lowest income quintile by about two-thirds, whereas they lowered the income share of the highest income group by about 12 percent. Taxes and transfers had little effect on the shares of the middle three quintiles but had larger effects on the highest and lowest quintiles. Taxes are the important effect in reducing the shares of the highest income group; transfers are the important effect in increasing the share of

TABLE 8   PRE- AND POST-TAX-TRANSFER INCOME
               DISTRIBUTION IN THE UNITED STATES, 1970

Income Quintile	Income share (percent)	
	Pre-Tax-Transfer	*Post-Tax-Transfer*
0–20	4.9	8.2
20–40	11.1	13.9
40–60	16.1	16.1
60–80	22.2	21.3
80–100	45.8	40.4

Source: Benjamin Okner, "Total U.S. Taxes and Their Effect on the Distribution of Family Income in 1966 and 1970," Table 8, in Henry Aaron and Michael Boskin (eds.), *The Economics of Taxation* (Washington, D.C.: Brookings Institution, 1980).

the lowest income group. The same study shows that the entire effect of taxes and transfers in reducing inequality came from federal government taxes and transfers.

Do taxes and transfers intended to redistribute income distort resource allocation. The answer must be yes. A tax-transfer system intended to produce an income distribution that is less unequal than the competitive distribution must make use of taxes and transfers that are systematically correlated with income. Experience in the United States and elsewhere shows that high marginal tax rates induce expenditures on legal and accounting services to enable taxpayers to avoid the highest tax rates. Such resource uses are a social waste. Tax evasion is also induced, which causes labor and other inputs to be deovted to activities whose returns, although lower than could be obtained, can be concealed from tax authorities. High marginal tax rates also distort choices between paid work and leisure. Although many labor economists doubt that the effect is large, do-it-yourself activities must be partly the result of high marginal taxes. Fringe benefits are largely the creation of high taxes and distort consumption expenditures and savings decisions. Sales, real estate, and many other taxes are levied unevenly on commodities and distort consumer spending. Estate and inheritance taxes both distort incentives to provide for heirs and induce socially wasteful expenditures on accountants and lawyers to avoid paying them. Finally, every major corporate resource allocation decision is affected by tax consequences.

Probably the largest distortions are from transfers. Table 8 shows that about 40 percent of the post-tax-transfer income of the bottom quintile came from federal transfers. Each of the bottom two quintiles received about 40 percent of all government transfer payments. That percentage is about the same for those under and over retirement age. It is inconceivable that the result is not lower output and earnings by recipients. The conclusion is strengthened by the observation that the post-tax-transfer income share of the lowest quintile rose by less than the increased transfers paid to them during the 1960s and 1970s. The resulting loss of output is a social waste. Likewise, transfer recipients also engage in evasion. They are induced to engage in activities whose returns can be concealed and thus do not result in loss of transfer receipts, even though the returns to their work are lower than they would be in other activities. The results are distorted resource allocations.

All the activities identified in the two preceding paragraphs are resource misallocations resulting from government tax and transfer programs. Nobody knows their total magnitude, but there should be no presumption that they are small. The point is not that government income redistribution is desirable or undesirable. Instead, the point is that government tax-transfer programs inevitably cause resource misallocation, or waste. A competitive income distribution is socially efficient because the resource allocation that generates it is socially efficient. It is impossible to interfere with the income distribution without affecting resource allocation. Some interferences with income distribution are more distorting than others. But large interferences always entail large distortions.[6]

OPTIMUM INCOME REDISTRIBUTION

How much, if any, income redistribution should governments undertake?

As stated in Chapter 1, the basic idea of welfare economics is that an economy should be organized so as to make people as well off as possible and that governments should intervene only insofar as it achieves that goal. This idea motivated the discussion regarding ways to make the economy socially efficient that was presented in Chapter 3. The fact that people's self-interest can be relied upon to place the economy on the utility frontier is what permits achievement of social efficiency with a minimum of government intervention. Government actions that are needed for the purpose can command unanimous or nearly unanimous support of citizens.

The foregoing suggests that attempts to alter the competitive distribution of income or well-being should be based on consensus among affected people. The difficulty is that, although social efficiency can be achieved without reducing anyone's well-being, income redistribution inevitably entails increasing some people's well-being at the expense of others'. Thus the presumption must be that consensus about equity issues is much weaker than consensus about social efficiency issues.

Nevertheless, economists and others have long based their analysis of optimum income redistribution on some concept of consensus. Starting one and a half centuries ago, utilitarian economists, especially John Stuart Mill, assumed that society should maximize the total well-being, or sum of utilities of, its members. During the last half century, economists have refined the utilitarian concept and introduced the notion of a social welfare function. In most formulations, it is assumed only that the social welfare function has a few simple characteristics, such as that it increases with each individual's well-being and perhaps decreases as inequality of well-being increases.

Most utilitarian formulations have an egalitarian orientation in that they conclude that governments should redistribute income toward equality until the loss of efficiency from government interference is so great that it more than offsets the value of the gains in equality. Although few are explicit on the subject, scholars vary as to the social inefficiency they believe should be tolerated to achieve greater equality.[7]

Despite many attempts, no one has ever proposed a persuasive method of comparing well-being of different people or a persuasive reason for assuming that there is or should be strong consensus on any criterion for government interference with income distribution. Thus applied studies of optimum income distribution assume social welfare functions that their authors believe to be plausible but that lack any empirical basis.[8] On the assumption that government actions must represent citizen consensus, at least in a democracy, some are tempted to estimate social welfare functions from data on income redistribution actually carried out. But to assume without evidence or analysis that what a democratic government does must be optimum is to deny the distinction between positive and normative analysis.

The extreme of the consensus view about income redistribution by government is the assumption that income redistribution is a public good.[9] The assumption is that the well-being of the nonpoor is improved by the knowledge that the poor are being assisted. If this is the case, redistribution can make everyone better off. The poor are made better off by the redistributed funds, and the nonpoor are made better off by knowledge that the poor are being helped.

If the nonpoor are made better off by knowledge that the poor are being helped, why do the nonpoor not undertake the redistribution themselves without government intervention? One answer is that they do, and would do more if governments did not undertake such large redistributions through tax-transfer programs.

But the issue is more complex and more subtle. To make the case for redistribution as a public good as strong as possible, consider the following example. Suppose there were no redistributive tax-transfer programs. Further suppose that society can be divided into two homogeneous groups, poor and nonpoor, with the latter group ten times as large as the former. Suppose, finally, that it would be worth at least $100 to each nonpoor family if it knew that each poor family's income were $1,000 larger. Then a redistribution program that taxed each nonpoor family $100 and transferred $1,000 to each poor family would be a pure public good. The nonpoor would benefit from knowing that the poor were being helped, so there would be no additional cost of benefiting an additional nonpoor family. Furthermore, the public good is nonexcludable, in that, if the transfer program took effect, no nonpoor family could be prevented from benefiting. Thus the transfer program would satisfy both criteria for a pure public good, and its enactment would command unanimous approval among both the poor and the nonpoor. Furthermore, as was shown in Chapter 3, nonexcludability creates the strongest case for government intervention in public-good production.

If this is a tolerable approximation to reality, why are redistribution programs so controversial? I believe there are two answers. First, although the principle of redistribution may command large support, the present amount of it may not. Rich countries, including the United States, tend to be compassionate. Most of us would be willing to pay our share of the cost of programs that prevent destitute poverty among residents. But programs that tax people of moderate incomes to provide large transfers to other people command much less support. Thus support falls off as the magnitude of the tax-transfer program rises. Second, most existing transfer programs are only poorly focused on the needy. People whose hard work generates moderate earnings are incensed at the notion that their taxes are used to provide transfers to others whose living standards are at comparable levels. Thus the consensus characteristic, or public-good aspect, of tax-transfer programs is strong but declines as the transfer programs become large and/or poorly focused on needy recipients.

The implication of this argument is that the controversial aspects of tax-transfer programs are quantitative. I believe that a modest government program well focused on needy people could command near-unanimous support. Redistributive programs that coerce large minorities are dangerous and divisive in a democracy.[10] That a modest and well-focused transfer program would command wide support is supported by evidence from public opinion polls and by evidence from voting behavior, but such evidence is notoriously unreliable. Several papers that take account of distorting effects of taxes and transfers on taxpayers and transfer recipients have estimated how much redistribution would maximize utilitarian social welfare functions. Such studies tend to be inconclusive, as Slemrod has shown, and they take no account of the destructive characteristics of a coercive transfer program.[11]

At this point, discussion of a specific program will help to fix magnitudes and clarify pros and cons.

A PROPOSAL FOR INCOME REDISTRIBUTION

During the 1960s and 1970s, economists did more work on poverty and on programs to redistribute income than on any other social issue. The program proposed here has been studied by many scholars.[12] The purpose here is to embody the proposal in recent data and to persuade readers how cheap, effective, and simple a well-designed program would be. The proposal is an example of a negative-income tax scheme.

The proposal is based on the following specific normative assumptions.

First, the program should eliminate destitute poverty. Present transfer programs spend large amounts of taxpayers' money but do not eliminate poverty. In 1982, government transfers represented more than 10 percent of GNP but left 15 percent of the population below the government poverty line. The more destitute the poverty to be eliminated, the stronger the consensus on this matter. The proposal to be presented here is quite generous, yet remarkably inexpensive.

Second, the program should replace all transfer programs. Present programs are large, complex, and diffuse. They have been put in place to help noisy or politically powerful groups. They bear no relationship to a coherent concept of income redistribution. The last thing the United States needs is another transfer program superimposed on existing programs. Specifically, the proposed program should replace all welfare programs, unemployment compensation, social security, medicare, medicaid, disability, food stamps, and educational assistance programs. In 1983, federal, state, and local governments spent $338.7 billion on such transfers to people.[13]

To be fair to present recipients, such programs would need to be replaced gradually. Those now receiving transfers would need to be allowed to continue doing so during their eligibility under present laws. Social security is the most difficult because it is contributory. A sensible transition would be to cease contributions from workers when the new transfer program came into effect. Those who had already contributed to social security during part of their working lives could be given the choice, upon retirement, between the new program and a modified social security program under which they would receive, in an actuarial sense, social security contributions made on their behalf cumulated at, say, a 1 or 2 percent real interest rate per year. Those already retired when the new program came into effect should be given the choice between continuing to collect social security under present laws and taking part in the new program. The implication is that the transition to the new program would probably take place over a period of 20 to 25 years.

Third, the program should be focused as much as possible on the poor. Its goal should be to help those who are destitute, not to insure against all of life's adverse contingencies. People should be expected to save against retirement, ill health, and unemployment. The program should prevent destitute poverty among those who are unable or unwilling to make superior provisions for themselves. It should not be so generous as to reduce substantially the incentive that people have to provide for themselves.

Fourth, the program should not provide transfers that enable recipients to achieve higher living standards than those not eligible for the transfer program. Nothing so demoralizes the modest-income, taxpaying public as transfer programs that enable recipients to live better than those who work and pay taxes.

Fifth, and finally, the program should provide incentive to recipients to substitute their earnings for transfers. An important problem with present transfer programs is that they entail great cost to recipients, in foregone transfer payments, if they increase their earnings. In many cases, a female-headed household with children—receiving aid to families with dependent children, medicaid, food stamps, and subsidized housing—may need to earn enough to place her family well above the official poverty line before increased earnings enable the family to improve its living standards. Because most poor people have poor work histories and little earning power, they are deterred from acquiring experience and work habits that enable them to become more productive and self-sufficient. Evidence collected from social experiments with negative-income tax programs suggests that these incentive effects may not be large.[14] In fact, one cannot be sure. Results of the negative-income tax experiments were confounded because, although most transfers were denied to beneficiaries, some of those with the worst incentive effects were continued. In addition, the transfers available under the experiments were known to be temporary. Even if the incentive effects of the program proposed here are modest, it is important to provide recipients the security of being able to revert to the transfer program if their efforts to become self-supporting should fail.

It should be pointed out that the third and fifth goals are in conflict. The best way to motivate higher earnings among transfer recipients is to reduce transfer payments by less than earnings increments at low earnings levels. In this way, increased earnings are rewarded by higher living standards. But this requires that substantial transfers be given to those above the level of destitute poverty. The only alternative to this incentive is detailed rules and policing as to eligibility in an attempt to exclude those who could earn enough to support themselves but choose not to. Such rules become complex, and policing entails degrading intrusion by government officials into the lives of transfer recipients. In the United States, experience indicates that policing is expensive and ineffective. By contrast, the only intrusion required by a negative-income tax program is auditing to verify earnings and family status. The required auditing is similar to that now required of income tax payers, and the negative-income tax and its auditing could be integrated with the income tax system.

A final comment is that some people will certainly be made worse off by substitution of a modest negative-income tax program for present transfer programs. Every dollar spent by governments benefits someone. Thus, although the proposed program would move society toward the utility frontier, it would also redistribute government transfers from less to more needy recipients. If the view is taken that all present transfer recipients deserve their present transfers, then discussion stops. But if the view is taken that the sole purpose of a government transfer system is to eliminate serious poverty by providing a guaranteed floor to living standards, with incentives for self-help and a minimum of government intrusion into recipients' lives, then it can be done for about half the cost of present transfer programs.

The proposal is illustrated with 1981 data and prices, the latest available at the time of writing. The proposal is that each adult be guaranteed an income of $250 per month at the 1981 price level and each child be guaranteed 60 percent as much, $150 per month.[15] The guarantee comes to $9,600 per year for a family of two adults and two children, somewhat above the official poverty line of $9,287 for 1981. A family would receive the guaranteed amount from the government if it had no income. For each dollar of private income, the government transfer would be reduced 50 cents.[16] Thus, a family of four would receive no transfer payment if it: annual income exceeded $19,200. Each year, the guaranteed amounts should increase proportionately with inflation. The guaranteed income represents about 25 percent of average personal income in 1981, and the transfer payment cutoff is at about 50 percent of average personal income.

Everyone would be eligible for this transfer (subject only to the conditions on income and family status just listed) but for no other government transfers. People could receive it permanently if they were poor or lazy, they could receive it temporarily if they were sick or unemployed, or they could use it to supplement private pensions.

How much would such a program cost? Table 9 shows calculated payments by income level for families in 1981. The first column shows the income brackets in which the source presents the data. Because higher income figures are not needed for present purposes, data are shown only for family incomes up to $20,000. The second column shows all money income less all government transfers per family for each income bracket. Averages including transfers, not shown, are close to bracket midpoints. That the averages excluding transfers are all at or below the lower ends of the brackets indicates how large and poorly focused existing transfers are. For example, in the highest bracket in the table, mean income including transfers is $18,725, implying that average transfers per family are $2,420 (equal to $18,725 − $16,305) even in this relatively high bracket. The third column shows the income guaranteed by the proposed negative-income tax plan for an average family in each income bracket. The numbers in the third column differ slightly from each other, but only because family size and age composition vary somewhat by income level. The fourth column shows the average transfer under the negative-income tax plan for a family in each bracket. The transfer is the amount in the third column minus half the amount in the second column. Transfer payments fall from $7,464 in the lowest bracket, in which transfers are now and would be under the proposed program almost the sole source of income, to zero at a family income above $17,500. The final column shows total income for each bracket, the sum of columns two and four.

The data in Table 9 are probably approximately accurate estimates of the cost of a negative-income tax for families based on the assumption that the program has no effect in stimulating earnings compared with existing transfer programs. Almost certainly, the proposed negative-income tax program would stimulate at least modest increases in earnings

TABLE 9   CALCULATED NEGATIVE-INCOME TAX
PAYMENTS TO U.S. FAMILIES, 1981
(Dollars per Year)

Gross Money Income Range	Money Income Less Existing Government Transfers per Family	Negative-Income Tax		
		Annual Guaranteed Income per Family	Annual Transfer	Government Transfer Plus Private Income
Less than $2,500	0	7,464	7,464	7,464
2,500–5,000	1,426	7,230	6,517	7,943
5,000–7,500	2,937	7,530	6,062	8,999
7,500–10,000	5,121	7,764	5,204	10,325
10,000–12,500	8,082	7,776	3,735	11,817
12,500–15,000	10,667	7,956	2,623	13,290
15,000–17,500	13,659	8,028	1,198	14,857
17,500–20,000	16,305	8,028	0	16,305

SOURCE: Calculated from data in *U.S. Census Bureau, Current Population Reports*, Series P-60, No. 137, March 1983 (Washington, D.C.: U.S. Department of Commerce, 1983) and from the formula described in this text.

in comparison with existing programs. In that case, the cost of the proposed program would be lower than that assumed in the table.

Two adjustments are needed to obtain the full cost of a negative-income tax program from the data in Table 9. First, the table applies only to families. In 1981, 198.3 million people lived in the country's 61.0 million families. In addition, there were 27.7 million unrelated individuals in the country. The census source shows their income levels, but not transfer sources; so transfers cannot be subtracted from incomes of unrelated individuals. A crude estimate is that 7.6 million unrelated individuals would collect about $10.2 billion under the proposed negative-income tax programs.[17] Second, people eligible for transfers under the proposed program now pay federal income and social security taxes. If their increased living standards are to be kept at 50 percent of their increased earnings, no positive income or social security tax can be collected from those who receive negative-income payments. In 1981, about $25.4 billion was collected in federal personal income taxes from those eligible for payments under the proposed program. Social security taxes were probably about the same amount.[18]

Total payments to families under the proposed transfer programs would be about $94.9 billion. Payments to unrelated individuals would be about $10.2 billion. Foregone federal personal income and social security taxes might be about $50 billion. Thus the full cost of the negative-income tax program in 1981 would be about $155 billion. Federal, state, and local government transfer payments in 1981 were $323.9 billion. Thus the cost of the proposed program would be somewhat less than half the cost of existing transfer payments programs.

Other assumptions can be made about program characteristics, about eligibility, and about incentive effects; and more careful calculations could be made. The point of the calculations is to illustrate a program that would have important advantages in comparison with present transfers. First, it would eliminate poverty as defined by government standards, whereas actual transfers left 15 percent of the country's population in poverty in 1982.[19] Second, it would raise living standards and eliminate federal tax payments for almost everyone whose income was less than about twice the poverty level. Third, it would provide stronger incentives for self-help than present transfer programs. Fourth, it would not provide transfers that permitted recipients to achieve living standards higher than those who worked and paid taxes. Fifth, the program would be simple and comprehensible to poor and nonpoor alike and could be administered inexpensively and with minimum intrusion into the lives of recipients, in conjunction with the federal personal income tax. Sixth, on pessimistic assumptions, it would cost no more than half as much as the present array of transfer programs.

CONCLUSIONS

This chapter has continued the welfare economic analysis of government activities, focusing on equity issues. The conclusion was reached that there is inevitably much less consensus about government actions to redistribute income or well-being than about government actions to improve social efficiency. The judgment was put forward that an effective program of income redistribution would command wide public support and that government intervention is justified because such a program has all the characteristics of a pure public good that make private provision infeasible. The judgment that the program would command support of the vast majority of citizens and would require only minimal coercion of a small minority is crucial for its success.

How much redistribution government should undertake depends on how much society wants to reduce inequality from that implied by the competitive distribution of income, on how much distortion in resource allocation of taxpayers and transfer recipients is to be tolerated, and on how much consensus there is on the subject among citizens.

An illustrative calculation showed that a simple negative-income tax program could eliminate involuntary poverty, improve incentives of the poor for self-help, and eliminate inequities in the present system of transfer payments. This immediately raises the question why we have the present system of cumbersome, complex, expensive, and poorly focused transfer payments. The answer must be that reducing poverty is no more than one of several goals of the present system. Other possible goals of the system are explored in Chapter 9, which is concerned with the positive theory of government.

FIVE

Unemployment, Inflation, Economic Growth, and Government Macroeconomic Policies

This book is mostly about microeconomic or general equilibrium aspects of government actions: about what kinds of government spending and other interventions are justified and the harmful effects of government actions that are not justified. However, no one should claim that domestic roles of governments should be reduced substantially without coming to grips with macroeconomic influences and policies of government.

Microeconomic aspects of government actions have received much attention by economists during recent decades. However, the great debate among economists, which started about the beginning of the second quarter of the twentieth century, has concerned macroeconomic issues. Should governments take responsibility to promote full employment and economic growth and to prevent inflation? If so, how? And how should conflicts among those three goals be reconciled?

Beyond doubt, several thousand scholarly books and papers have been published on this subject in the United States alone since the late 1920s, and this output has probably been matched abroad. Until the early 1950s, England was the scene of most of the intellectual ferment on the subject, and to this day, the air there is warmed by such controversy.

Until the late 1960s, a consensus on major issues seemed to be emerging slowly among macroeconomists. Since then, opposing groups, identified as Keynesians, post-Keynesians, monetarists, rational expectationists, and structuralists, and by other appellations, have emerged. The popular identification of such groups as *schools of thought* gives an erroneous impression of precision and clarity. *Potpourri* is a more apt term.

I make no pretense of settling these issues here. My goal is only to step lightly on the periphery of the fray to indicate what seem to be relatively noncontroversial aspects of appropriate macroeconomic policies, especially as they relate to the sizes and functions of governments. The basic point is that nothing in economic logic or evidence indicates that the best macroeconomic policy requires governments to be larger or to perform more functions than those that have been indicated in Chapters 3 and 4. Appropriate government stabilization and growth policies do not require that governments be larger than is justified on microeconomic grounds. Indeed, it is suggested later in this chapter that appropriate macroeconomic policy would be simpler if governments intervened less in microeconomic affairs of the economy.

The term *macroeconomic policies* is used here to refer to monetary and fiscal policies; basically, to policies that set levels and growth rates of money supply, government spending, and government taxing and borrowing. Such policies are sometimes referred to as *stabilization policies.* Other government policies are classified as *microeconomic* in this book. Also, in this macroeconomics chapter, as throughout the book, I restrict consideration to domestic issues.

WHAT IS THE
MACROECONOMIC PROBLEM?

In order to place bounds on justifiable government stabilization policies, it is necessary to spell out the nature of the macroeconomic problem. It is best to start with a brief review of how and why economies create jobs.

Suppose, to focus the argument, that no one were employed doing valuable work. Then nothing that people want or need would be produced. People would quickly perceive that work would make available commodities they want and that the utility resulting from consumption of the resulting commodities would exceed the disutility of the work. People would hunt, farm, and mine to extract materials from the environment, and they would then process the materials into useful commodities: food, clothing, shelter, and other products. What would be produced would depend on tastes for commodities, what technology of production is known, and what can be found in the environment, and so forth.

Workers would realize that specialization pays. They would devote themselves to production of a narrow range of commodities, which they would trade for other commodities with workers specializing in their production. Companies, some of them large, would be organized to take advantage of scale economies and related phenomena. Legal arrangements would be needed to provide for companies employing more than a few workers, and money would be needed to facilitate exchange in a specialized economy.

Each worker wishes to work a number of hours per week such that the value of additional commodities and services that individual can obtain by additional work equals the disutility of the additional work. For a worker employed for money wages, the additional commodities and services resulting from additional work are the ones valued most highly among those that can be bought with the extra money earned.

In a specialized economy in which workers are hired by firms, a demand side to the labor market must also be considered. Firms are started in lines of activity in which profits can be made—that is, in which products can be sold at prices adequate to cover minimum production costs, including costs of needed amounts and kinds of capital. A profit-seeking firm employs a number of workers for a number of hours each, such that neither more nor less employment or hours can generate larger profit. Hours of work cannot be adjusted entirely on the basis of the desires of individual workers because employers must employ many workers for a coherent work period.

The interaction between labor supply and demand provides each worker with the amount of work that worker desires, subject to the need for coherent work periods by employers. In terms of welfare economics, it is easy to show that the assumptions made in Chapters 1 and 3 imply that the labor market model just outlined ensures that the economy is on the utility frontier. No change in wages or employment can make any group of workers better off without making others worse off. Only minor modifications are required of this model to take account of voluntary and other nonprofit organizations that might be needed to generate socially efficient production.

In this model, there is no involuntary unemployment. If there are people for whom the utility of extra consumption made possible by work exceeds the disutility of the work, it is profitable for firms to hire them. For any of several reasons, many people may choose not to work for pay. For example, for some people, especially mothers of small children, the utility of childcare and other household production may exceed the utility that can be obtained from the extra commodities available because of paid work. But with the approximation just noted, people work as much as they want to at wages representing their productivity. Even hours of work are remarkably flexible. Many workers have, and most workers can have, flexible hours, part-time work, or multiple jobs; so they can adjust their hours of work to their precise preferences.

Thus, on the most abstract level, there is nothing to discuss in this chapter. The government actions that are sufficient to enable the private economy to be socially efficient ensure, among other things, full employment of the labor force. If government restricts itself to the justifiable actions outlined in Chapter 3, profit-seeking or nonprofit institutions are motivated to employ anyone willing to work at a wage that reflects that individual's productivity.

Although the exposition has been brief, this model is an accurate description of the way labor markets work for about 90 percent of the 110 million U.S. residents who are in the labor force. For those 90 percent, labor markets would work even better if governments would permit them to. Although they are far from perfect, most labor markets work well and produce a socially efficient allocation of the economy's most valuable resource: its trained and specialized labor force. People too often think of labor markets as being dominated by a few large and inflexible industrial firms and unions. Fewer than 20 percent of workers are employed in manufacturing, and many of those are employed in small firms. About the same percentage of workers belongs to unions. Most workers are employed in a large variety of service industries. Altogether, there are about 15 million firms in the United States, not to mention the uncounted thousands of nonprofit employers and nearly 10 million self-employed workers.[1]

Analysis of macroeconomic stabilization policies is built around the notion that labor markets do not work well for 5 or 10 percent of the labor force. During the 1970s, the measured civilian unemployment rate was more than 5 percent of the labor force in almost all years and was more than 10 percent in some months. Why? Some distinctions are needed.

The concept of unemployment is inherently fuzzy. To say that is not to make light of the problem. In the United States, adults are counted as unemployed if they are not working and are actively seeking work.

First, some people not working want to work, but not at wages that reflect their productivity. They may continue seeking work more or less indefinitely and may eventually accept employment as they lower their standards as to what is acceptable or likely to materialize. Such unemployment is a luxury of those with other means of support, but there is some in an affluent society such as the United States. Some people with employed spouses and some young people living with employed parents are in this category.

Second, and more important, some of those recorded as unemployed are transitional, moving from one job to another. As consumer demands and technology change, and as workers move through the life cycle, job changes are inevitable. In a large and specialized economy, matching workers and jobs is a subtle and time-consuming process. Some workers can search for a new job while working at the old one; others quit or are laid off before finding a new job. The latter group constitutes part of the unemployed. If unemployed, how long one searches before accepting a new job depends on how scarce jobs are, but it also depends on how important it is to find work quickly. One's tolerance of unemployment while seeking work depends on one's nerves and on one's family status and assets. For example, people with working spouses can and do search longer than others. Likewise, young people who have finished school search longer if their parents support them until they find work. The latter group has been especially large during the late 1970s and early 1980s as the postwar baby boom has entered the labor force. New entrants take longer than others to find jobs because they are inexperienced at both search and work. The concept of transitional unemployment is fuzzy at the edges, but it is clear that many unemployed people are transitionally unemployed in the United States. It is also clear that the distinction between transitional and chronic unemployment is important. There is a world of difference between the situation of a 21-year-old college graduate who spends the summer after graduation looking for just the right job and that of a 58-year-old with a tenth grade education whose job has disappeared because of automation.

Nobody knows how many people counted as unemployed are in the two categories just identified. The most careful estimates place the number at 4 to 6 percent of the labor force.[2] The share of the labor force in these categories has certainly risen since the 1950s, when the measured unemployment rate was frequently below 4 percent. One reason is larger percentages of young and female labor force entrants and participants. Another reason is that increased affluence and numbers of two-worker families have made long job searches more tolerable. The two categories are referred to here as voluntary and transitional unemployment.

Voluntary and transitional unemployment cannot be much affected by macroeconomic stabilization policies. Job searches are certainly shorter during prosperous times, but the unemployment rate that is immune to government stabilization policies is probably not less than 4 percent. Five percent may be the best estimate. Unemployment in excess of 5 percent of the labor force is not necessarily small. In 1982 and 1983, the measured civilian unemployment rate was in excess of 10 percent for ten consecutive months. During that period, unemployment exceeded 5 percent of the labor force by about 5 million people. Although that was the worst period since the 1930s, even less unemployment represents a substantial sacrifice of output, income, and human dignity.

It is deeply discouraging that macroeconomic specialists are still divided as to the basic causes of involuntary unemployment. Some believe that the private economy is inherently unstable and that large fluctuations in employment, output, and prices can be prevented only by government monetary and fiscal policies that are fine tuned to the ups and downs of the private economy. Others believe that economic fluctuations result mainly from government monetary and fiscal actions. Finally, some destabilizing shocks certainly originate abroad. The best recent examples are the oil shocks in 1973 and 1979.

MACROECONOMIC POLICIES

Through most of the post–World War II period, the vast majority of macroeconomists have claimed that government could stimulate the private economy by large government spending and low tax yields. Resulting deficits must be financed either by net issuance of government bonds or by increases in the money supply. All economists have realized that sufficiently great government spending or deficits would be inflationary, and there has been prolonged debate as to how much inflation should be tolerated to get unemployment down and what combination of large spending, low taxes, money supply growth, and government bond growth should be employed to achieve that goal. As a result, in recent years, this large consensus has broken down.

This broadly Keynesian view of macroeconomic policy was gradually adopted by the national government. Although few macroeconomists would agree that the national government has ever followed a precise Keynesian policy, the need to stimulate the economy has been increasingly used to justify large spending, deficits, and tax cuts. The key political commitment was the Employment Act of 1946, but the federal government became explicitly and aggressively committed to monetary and fiscal policies to stimulate the economy during the early 1960s.

A brief summary of macroeconomic trends and government policies is presented in Table 10. The first three columns display three major objects of government stabilization policy: the unemployment rate, the inflation rate, and the growth rate of output per hour (or labor productivity) in the business sector of the economy. The last three columns present

TABLE 10   AVERAGES OF MAJOR MACROECONOMIC VARIABLES, 1950–1983

	Unemployment Rate[a]	Inflation Rate[b]	Productivity Growth[c]	Government Spending as Percent of GNP[d]	Government Deficit as Percent of GNP[e]	Money Supply Growth[f]
1950–1954	4.0	2.4	3.7	25.5	0.2	3.5
1955–1959	5.0	1.6	2.7	26.2	0.2	1.6
1960–1964	5.7	1.2	3.3	27.9	0.2	2.6
1965–1969	3.8	3.3	2.5	29.5	0.3	4.9
1970–1974	5.4	5.9	1.6	31.5	0.5	6.0
1975–1979	7.0	7.7	1.4	32.4	1.1	6.8
1980–1983	8.5	7.9	1.1	34.4	2.6	7.3

SOURCES: U.S. Council of Economic Advisers, Economic Report to the President (Washington, D.C.: U.S. Government Printing Office, 1975 and 1984).

[a]Unemployment rate is the arithmetic mean of annual average civilian unemployment rates.

[b]Inflation rate is the compound percent growth rate of the consumer price index.

[c]Productivity growth is the compound growth rate, real output per hour, business sector.

[d]Government spending is the arithmetic mean of total government spending, including transfers, as percent of GNP, income and product accounts.

[e]Deficit is arithmetic mean of total government deficit, counting surpluses as negative deficits, as percent of GNP, income and product accounts.

[f]Money supply growth is compound growth rate of M_1, currency and checkable deposits.

three series that government uses to attempt to stabilize the economy: government spending and the government deficit, both presented as percentages of GNP, and the growth rate of the money supply.[3]

Annual data are inappropriate to measure changes in government policies. Throughout the period covered by Table 10, spending on government transfer programs, such as unemployment compensation, has risen automatically during recessions. Likewise, federal government tax receipts fall faster than GNP during recessions because of the progressivity of federal income taxes. Thus annual variables may be the results as well as the causes of economic stability or fluctuations. During a five-year period, upturns and downturns average out to a considerable extent, and data can reveal underlying trends in government policies and in their effects.

Table 10 shows dramatic and progressive failure of government stabilization policies. During the latest four years covered, the unemployment rate was more than twice as high as during the first five years covered, the inflation rate was three times as great, and the growth rate of productivity had fallen by two-thirds. The last three columns show increasingly aggressive use of government stimulatory policies. Total government spending as a share of GNP grew by one-third during the period covered by the table, the annual government deficit grew ten times as a percentage of GNP, and the annual growth rate of the money supply doubled.

Rapidly rising government spending and deficits and accelerating money supply growth have been accompanied by deteriorating macro performance of the economy, unemployment and inflation have worsened, and productivity growth has slowed. Table 10 certainly does not prove that growth of governments has been the sole cause of the deterioration in macro performance of the U.S. economy. But the best analyses of the deterioration in U.S. economic performance agree that the acceleration of inflation, rising interest rates, and instability that governments have caused or worsened have been among the important causes of poor recent performance of the U.S. economy.[4]

Rising government deficits and faster money supply growth have made inflation worse than previously without reducing unemployment or stimulating economic growth or productivity advances. Large government expenditures have absorbed scarce resources needed by the private economy and have failed to reduce unemployment. Rising government deficits have also absorbed increasing amounts of private savings needed to finance private capital formation and have forced up real interest rates. Most important of all, the increasing variability of government spending, government deficits, and money supply growth have destabilized the economy and increased the difficulty and riskiness of private market planning. Finally, the increased regulation of the economy that has inevitably accompanied growth of governments has reduced the adaptability and flexibility of the private economy—specifically, its ability to create new jobs quickly in response to changing conditions.

The claims made in the previous paragraph are not particularly controversial among macroeconomists. No thoughtful economist doubts that excessive government spending absorbs resources that could be used by the private sector, that rapid growth of the money supply has contributed to inflation, that large government deficits have forced up real interest rates, or that government regulation has increased since the 1960s and has reduced the flexibility of the economy. How much of the deterioration in the macro performance of the U.S. economy can be explained by these government actions is controversial. But the key point is that these macro policies have produced no benefits in economic performance.

APPROPRIATE MONETARY
FISCAL POLICIES

During much of the period from 1950 to the early 1970s, many macroeconomists believed that mildly inflationary government policy would promote full employment and economic growth without harmful effects on the economy. The argument has been that government deficits, financed to a considerable extent by increases in the money supply, would stimulate output and employment when there was slack in the economy. It was believed that such fiscal and monetary policies could keep the economy close to full employment with no more than mild inflationary effects. As the economy approached full employment and inflation accelerated, it was felt that the deficits should vanish, or nearly vanish, and the growth of the money supply should be slowed.

Economists differed as to how much inflation they thought was necessary or tolerable to achieve low unemployment rates. But most economists thought that government should err on the side of risking inflation instead of substantial unemployment. Unemployment meant loss of real output and income, whereas mild inflation was thought to be approximately costless, or at worst, to be a small price to pay to promote high levels of employment.

This is a brief and inadequate account of the Keynesian view of appropriate fiscal and monetary policies.[5] Macroeconomists sympathetic to the Keynesian view differ in their evaluation of postwar fiscal and monetary policies. More important, it is impossible to know to what extent Keynesian analysis has influenced government macro policies. It will be claimed in Chapter 9 that government monetary and fiscal policies have been only loosely related to any coherent view of stabilization policies. Nevertheless, it is indisputable that Keynesian analysis was increasingly influential in both the executive and legislative branches of the national government during the 1950s, 1960s, and early 1970s.

The most charitable view of fiscal and monetary policies during the 1970s and early 1980s is that the federal government failed to understand that inflation is like drugs: Small doses work at first, but larger and larger doses are gradually required to obtain the same effect, until eventually the victim dies.

Inflationary monetary and fiscal policies stimulate increases in production and real incomes only so long as people fail to anticipate the inflation and are therefore willing to lend and invest at low or negative real rates of return. There is no other way that inflation can stimulate the economy. If funds are available at negative real interest rates, producers are induced to invest and commit resources to production, thus stimulating output and employment. If people correctly anticipate inflation, they invest only if money rates of return are high enough to maintain the real value of their assets intact and provide a real return. Roughly speaking, money interest rates adjust to an unchanging real rate plus the rate of inflation. This is not to say that the real rate of return never changes. It is affected by many events. It is to say only that it is not substantially affected by anticipated inflation.

For many years during the gradually accelerating postwar inflation, people were fooled about likely future inflation rates, partly because government continually promised price stability. For at least two decades, accelerating inflation and rising interest rates took people by surprise. Gradually, people learned that they had been investing at rates of return that reduced the real value of their assets. Money interest rates gradually rose, and government had to accelerate the rate of inflation to obtain a given economic stimulus. By the early 1980s, people had apparently learned their lesson well, and lenders had become so sensitive to inflation rates, that premiums were added to interest rates (making them well above inflation rates) because of the possibility that inflation might be worse than anticipated.

Table 10 shows the increasingly inflationary nature and effects of postwar monetary and fiscal policies. The next issue to be discussed is the mechanisms by which inflation causes the economy's macro performance to deteriorate.

The fundamental function of prices is to facilitate comparisons among possible transactions. This simple-sounding observation refers to crucial economic issues, such as job search, home ownership decisions, retirement arrangements, planning by large and small businesses, and investment planning as well as to ordinary consumer spending. All important economic decisions by households and businesses entail price comparisons. When prices change rapidly and unpredictably, such calculations become difficult or impossible. Even if inflation were a known and constant percentage per year, it would reduce the efficiency and raise the costs of careful planning. However, as has been seen, a constant rate of inflation is almost beyond the capability of governments. Once inflation starts, governments inevitably accelerate it to try to stimulate the economy in an attempt to offset the disincentive effects of inflation on employment and investment. Eventually, when inflation becomes very fast, governments panic and adopt stringent monetary and fiscal policies and frequently impose price and wage controls and other regulations intended to hold prices down. The result is that inflationary economies are almost inevitably economies with erratic price behavior and with a diverse set of government interferences that reduce economic efficiency.

Efficient planning becomes impossible in such situations. The result is that investment, employment, and growth all suffer. Both firms and households become increasingly unwilling to make long-term resource commitments. The worst example of this process in twentieth-century U.S. economic history was the 1981–82 recession, when the federal government and the Federal Reserve Board became determined to squeeze inflationary expectations out of the economy at the cost of about 5 million involuntarily unemployed people and an enormous loss of output. It is probable that there was no easier way to get the economy back on an even keel, but governments cannot impose such costs on the economy very often. When governments cause such erratic macroeconomic performance, it inevitably leads to demands for import controls, domestic regulation to reduce the effects of competition, and increased transfers to relieve the burdens imposed on people.

In extreme cases of inflation and resulting economic instability and stagnation, people abandon currencies and make transactions on a barter basis or with more stable foreign currencies. The United States has not yet arrived at such an extreme situation, but the economy has paid a terrible price in instability and slow growth for the erratic inflation that government has imposed.

Even if it were possible for governments to fool people for long periods and get them to accept negative real rates of return by inflating the economy, it would surely be the most cynical domestic policy that democratic governments follow. The main purpose of economic growth is to provide the living standards and security that come with prosperity. Even successful government inflationary policies cause people's accumulated savings to evaporate. The result is that efforts to provide for security against unemployment, illness, and retirement are frustrated.

Both large and rapidly growing government spending and excessive growth of the money supply are culprits in the self-defeating government attempts to stimulate the economy by inflation. Large government spending inevitably absorbs resources that could be better used by the private sector and induces governments to spend money on wasteful projects and harmful regulation of the private sector. All such effects are inflationary. Large government spending tempts governments to attempt to hide the costs of its programs by financing with deficits instead of with painful taxes. Bond financing of deficits drives up interest rates because governments must compete with private borrowers for the supply of savings. Governments dislike bond-financed deficits because rapidly growing interest-bearing debt is visible and embarrassing and the large interest payments are an inflexible drain on government funds. People are disturbed because high interest rates depress durable goods industries, especially production of housing, business capital, and automobiles. Thus governments are tempted to finance deficits by rapid growth of the money supply. Although the result is certainly inflationary and disruptive of the economy, the connection is difficult for voters and taxpayers to establish. The costs of deficits financed by money supply growth do not appear on citizens' tax bills, and governments blame the resulting inflation on irresponsible or greedy segments of the private sector.

Inflationary fiscal and monetary policies cannot succeed for more than a few years. In the longer run, they must have devastating effects on the private economy, as experience in the United States—and to an even greater extent elsewhere—shows. Their most harmful long-run effect is that the poor macro performance of the economy they cause is blamed on the private sector and is used as a justification for even more government controls and spending. This has strong implications for the broad outlines of justifiable monetary and fiscal policies.

First, as indicated in Chapters 3 and 4, government spending should be determined by social efficiency and equity. There is no reason whatsoever to believe that large, growing, or accelerating government expenditures contribute to economic growth or full employment, however they are financed. Justifiable macroeconomic policies to stabilize the economy can be carried out as well by small governments as by large ones. Every dollar of government spending on goods and services means one dollar less of resources that can be allocated by the private economy; the opportunity cost of one dollar of government spending on goods and services is one dollar of reduced spending by the private sector.

Given government spending, taxes should be set so as to maintain approximate price stability. My own guess is that the implication of that rule is that tax policy should attempt to balance the government's budget. But macroeconomic research has not settled the issue whether instability originating outside the government might be mitigated by tax increases when inflation threatens and by decreases when deflation and unemployment threaten. The first priority with taxing and spending policies is to eliminate instability that originates in government fiscal and monetary policies. The issue is certainly not whether, other things being equal, inflation is worse than unemployment. Rather, the issue is that inflationary fiscal and monetary policies make unemployment worse, not better. They also lead inevitably to demands for more government spending and controls, which decrease the efficiency of the private economy. Provided government maintains approximate price stability and avoids regulation of labor and other markets, there is no economic analysis or evidence that indicates that the private economy will fail to generate jobs for all who wish to work at wages consistent with their productivity. All remaining unemployment would be voluntary or transitional. As discussed in Chapter 4, a well-focused system of transfer payments would drastically reduce the suffering resulting from any unemployment that might remain.

Budgets that are approximately balanced have an additional and important advantage: They enable taxpayer-voters to calculate the true cost of government and therefore to make more nearly rational political choices about government spending. Large deficit financing gives citizens the illusion that government spending is costless. This issue is discussed further in Chapter 9.

Monetary policy should be set in conjunction with fiscal policy so as to promote a stable price level. This requires gradual increases in the money supply so as to meet the needs of a growing economy.

Most important of all, government fiscal and monetary policies should be predictable and consistent. When changes are needed in government spending and taxing and in the money supply, they should be gradual and predictable. Predictability can be increased by announcements in advance of tax and spending actions as well as by consistent government responses to events. Small tax reductions when deflation and unemployment materialize permit the private sector to predict such tax reductions whenever they see or predict deflationary pressures.

Of the ideas presented here, perhaps the most difficult for many people to accept is that the private economy will generate jobs for all those who wish to work at wages that reflect their productivity if government macro policies follow the pattern indicated here. Full employment here means no unemployment, except for modest amounts of voluntary and short-lived transitional unemployment.

In poor countries, large amounts of employment are in what is referred to as the *informal sector*. In such activities, people offer services directly—transporting goods by hand, conveying messages, or providing other menial services. Some such work is performed, especially in slums, in the United States. Almost all informal sector work is poorly paid. Its defining characteristics are the absence of tools, machinery, and other capital equipment and absence of employment at ensured wages. Formal sector employment, almost the total of employment in the United States, requires investment. Buildings must be rented or bought, equipment must be acquired, a labor force must be assembled and paid, and production and marketing must be organized. These characteristics are present whether the employer is a billion dollar corporation or a new firm employing five or ten workers. Almost all well-paid and stable jobs are in such organizations. The key requirement to motivate such firms is the prospect of a competitive return on the investment. That prospect is impaired by excessive taxation, the prospect of inflation or economic instability, or the prospect that government will impose excessive costs by regulation.

The emphasis in this section has been on government macroeconomic policies that generate inflation and instability, increasing the private sector's difficulty in doing the economic planning that generates jobs. Large governments use resources that would be more productive in private use. But they do not make it inherently difficult for the private sector to employ remaining resources fully. Anytime there are unemployed people willing to work at wages that reflect their productivity, profit can be made by providing them jobs. A variety of government microeconomic policies makes it illegal or cumbersome for the private sector to create jobs for those who want to work at wages that reflect productivity.

INTERACTIONS BETWEEN GOVERNMENT MACRO AND MICRO POLICIES

Many economists and others are inclined to believe that the foregoing argument is fine in theory but cannot work in practice. The contention is that, because of rigidities in the private economy (especially in labor markets), full employment requires both inflationary fiscal and monetary policies and a variety of microeconomic interventions by governments. Many such rigidities are alleged, but perhaps the most common and deeply held belief is that workers no longer accept cuts in money or perhaps even in real wages. Beyond doubt, cuts in real wages are sometimes needed for groups of workers. Examples are when comparative advantage has shifted from the United States to other countries and an industry is forced to contract or disappear, when technical change causes decreased employment in an industry or occupation, or when—perhaps because of union activity—wages have simply reached unsustainable levels. During the 1970s and early 1980s, the first example occurred in the steel industry, the second with telephone operators, and the third in the automobile industry. In such cases, either money wages must fall or government must adopt one of two policies if it is determined not to allow employment to contract. First, it can keep money wages artificially high by micro interventions, such as import controls, direct or indirect subsidies, or restraining domestic competition. Second, it can inflate the economy by monetary and fiscal policies. Then the needed fall in real wages can be accomplished if money wages rise by less than the price level. In the United States, both strategies are followed by governments.

There are several answers to this contention.

First, inflationary monetary and fiscal policies have no better prospect of reducing real wages than they have of stimulating investment. Reductions in real wages are painful whether they take place by reductions of money wages with a constant price level or by an inflation rate that is faster than money wage increases. It insults the intelligence of workers to believe they can be fooled by such tricks for very long. Like other economic agents, organized workers have gradually learned during the period of accelerating inflation that money wages must rise as fast as prices if living standards are to be maintained. Attempts by governments to lower real wages by inflation are as self-defeating as attempts to stimulate investment and production by inflation. Neither can work for longer than a few years.

Second, money wage cuts do occur, as the 1981–82 recession made clear. Workers are naturally more loathe to accept money wage cuts when present and anticipated inflation is 5 or 10 percent than when prices are stable. Thus inflationary government policies themselves are a major deterrent to acceptance of money wage cuts. Also, the closer the economy is to full employment, the fewer and smaller the money wage cuts that will be necessary. Near full employment, other jobs can be found if one source of labor demand declines. Thus only small wage cuts are needed. Government inflationary policies that slow real growth and cause unemployment make more and larger real wage cuts necessary than would be necessary if government adopted more sensible macroeconomic policies.

Third, periods of unemployment would be less devastating if the federal government had a more efficient and equitable system of transfer payments. Reform, such as that suggested in Chapter 4, would reduce the cost of unemployment to those who lost their jobs. If the national government had an efficient and equitable system of transfer payments, it could adopt fiscal and monetary policies good for long-run efficiency of the economy without the need to protect every important industry and labor group from every threat to its economic position.

Finally, reduced government controls over the economy, especially over labor markets, would improve the flexibility of the economy. In the United States, governments impose an enormous variety of controls on labor and other markets. Especially in urban areas, federal, state, and local governments require large numbers of permits and licenses to be obtained, many regulatory conditions to be met, and much expense to be incurred before new or expanded facilities can employ workers and produce commodities. Such controls drastically reduce the ability of the economy to respond quickly to change. New industries cannot grow rapidly in response to new technology, shifts in demand, and changes in comparative advantage. Resources cannot move quickly from activities in which opportunities decline and to those that should expand. Investments needed to generate jobs are slowed or prevented. The result is to make unemployment longer and more frequent and to increase the temptation for more government microeconomic controls. Inevitably, persistent unemployment tempts government to try to stimulate the economy in the destructive ways described earlier in this chapter. In fact, to a considerable extent, the unemployment is caused by excessive government controls on economic activity.

Specific regulatory programs discussed in Chapters 6 and 7 illustrate this problem.

SIX

The Burden of Federal Government Regulation

Previous chapters have been concerned with excessive government spending and with the loss of social efficiency and equity that results. Such spending imposes large amounts of waste on the economy each year. Unfortunately, excessive spending is not the only (and perhaps not the most important) waste that governments impose on people. Although spending only relatively small amounts of money for the purpose, governments impose large amounts of waste on the economy by excessive and misguided regulation of private activities. Basically, government regulations prevent resources from being employed in ways that yield the highest monetary or direct utility returns to their owners. If government regulations do not affect the ways resources are used, they have no effect and can be withdrawn. An example is a maximum price that is set above the market equilibrium. It affects neither supply nor demand and thus has no effect on resource allocation.

But the purpose of government regulations is to affect resource allocation. Thus, except when governments make mistakes, regulations do affect resource allocation. Then they are said to be binding. Only binding regulations are economically relevant, and the adjective is implicit in this chapter.

Binding regulations are good examples of government use of its coercive power as discussed in Chapter 3, where it was suggested that coercion by governments can result in a move toward the utility frontier in only very special circumstances. Whether any existing federal regulatory programs satisfy those circumstances is discussed later in this chapter. If regulatory programs are unjustified, they impose on the private sector costs in the form of lower returns on productive resources and loss of consumer welfare that result from the regulation. For example, gasoline price controls during the 1970s kept the gasoline supply below the volume it would have attained in the absence of controls. Fewer resources were devoted to exploration for petroleum and to gasoline production than would have been devoted to those uses in the absence of the price controls. Such resources were used for other purposes (including, as a special case, the possibility that they were unemployed) in which social returns were lower than in petroleum exploration and gasoline production. Private returns were kept down by the price controls. One part of the social cost of gasoline price controls was the lower returns to labor, capital, and other inputs kept out of petroleum and gasoline production by the regulations.

The second part of the cost of excessive regulations is loss of consumer welfare. By virtue of gasoline price controls and the resulting shortages, consumers were forced to allocate resources to activities, including purchase of other goods and services and such activities as waiting in line or paying people to wait in line for scarce gasoline, that contributed less to their utility than more gasoline purchases would have.

The first of these losses—reduced returns to productive resources— is referred to as loss of producer surplus. It results in lower returns to owners of productive resources. The second loss—reduced utility to consumers from given expenditures of money and effort—is referred to as loss of consumer surplus. The sum of losses of producer and consumer surpluses represents the total direct loss of social efficiency from excessive regulation. Because all productive resources are owned by people who are also consumers, consumers bear all the social costs of excessive regulations. Losses of producer and consumer surplus are borne by the same people. The concepts simply provide a convenient classification of losses incurred on the supply and demand sides of the market. The loss of producer surplus does not depend on whether corporations, partnerships, proprietorships, or nonprofit institutions are the objects of regulation.

Economists know how to measure producer and consumer surplus, and they are estimated frequently in studies of benefits and costs of government intervention in economic activity. When regulatory programs have the effect of slowing or preventing innovation or adaptability of firms to changing conditions, losses of consumer and producer surplus are more difficult to measure. In such cases, the resulting loss of social efficiency stretches over many years and is difficult to trace back to particular regulations. Perhaps the most dramatic example is excessive regulation of innovation in prescription drugs.[1] The major cost is borne by people who would have lived longer or healthier lives if new drugs had become available more quickly. But no one can possibly know how many, which, or when drugs would have become available or who would have been saved from what illness if regulation had not been excessive. In many cases, measuring the loss of social efficiency when regulation slows innovation is not practically possible.

In addition to loss of consumer and producer surplus, two other categories of costs of government regulation complete the total. First is government administrative costs. Every government regulatory program requires government employees to administer it. Second is employment of resources by firms and consumers in their efforts to comply with the regulations. For example, gasoline companies must employ people to comply with price control programs. In practice, private compliance costs are difficult to distinguish from loss of producer surplus. The social loss from administrative and compliance costs is the commodities that could have been produced by resources employed to administer and comply with regulations. Most such costs are labor costs, and they are approximated by wages paid to those employed for the purpose.

The full social cost of regulatory programs is the sum of losses of producer and consumer surpluses plus administrative costs plus compliance costs. Regulation is socially beneficial only if the social benefits exceed the sum of the four social costs.

A CATALOG OF FEDERAL GOVERNMENT
REGULATORY PROGRAMS

Although federal regulation of consumer and, especially, producer activities is extremely pervasive and complex, no human being fully understands the entire spectrum of federal regulatory programs. All that can be done here is to peel one or two layers of skin off the onion by laying out major regulatory programs in a general way. State and local government regulatory programs are considered in Chapter 7.

The first thing to be said is that it is not clear in principle where the regulatory programs start and end. Most programs typically identified as regulatory have been legislated for the purpose of regulating private activities. But some regulatory programs are incidental to other federal programs. The most important example is tax collection. Tax laws contain myriad provisions as to what is taxed and how. They also spawn an enormous regulatory program as to how firms and individuals must keep their accounts and other records. Such regulatory programs are very important and impose large costs on taxpayers. Almost no one—lawyers, accountants, economists, or taxpayers—doubts that taxes are needlessly complex and that they have spawned needlessly complex and intrusive regulations. Indeed, the positive theory of government discussed in Chapter 9 could be applied as well to governments' tax programs and regulations as it can to their expenditures. Nevertheless, regulations spawned by tax laws are, in principle, incidental to a legitimate government activity: tax collection. Such regulations are not the main focus of this chapter.

The story of regulations spawned by government programs that have other goals could be repeated endlessly. Health care is another good example. Government programs to subsidize many aspects of health care have spawned an enormous regulatory apparatus. But the major purpose of the programs—medicare, medicaid, programs to finance hospital equipment purchases, and so forth—is subsidization, not regulation. In fact, regulation is endemic to government spending. Large spending programs invariably lead to regulation. It is not possible to have large government spending programs—whether in health, agriculture, education, or any other area—without large and intrusive accompanying regulatory programs. But the reverse is not true. Regulations can be, and are, imposed without large amounts of government spending. Here, attention is focused on regulations that are not incidental to other activities, not because such incidental regulations are necessarily less damaging or excessive, but because they require separate and extensive discussion.

Federal regulatory programs fall naturally into two groups, those put into place before and after World War II. Most prewar regulatory programs pertain to specific industries. Others, specifically the antitrust laws, apply to all but a few industries. Regulatory programs put into place since World War II mostly pertain to specific economic activities that are common to all, or most, industries. One postwar regulatory act, the Taft-Hartley Act, is included in the prewar list because it fits most easily into prewar categories of regulation.

Pre–World War II Regulation

Table 11 provides a list of major prewar federal regulatory programs. Each entry lists a basic act of Congress, the year it was passed, and the regulatory program it mandates. Only major acts with broad applications

TABLE 11   PRE–WORLD WAR II FEDERAL
                REGULATORY PROGRAMS

Legislation		Scope
1887	Act to Regulate Commerce	Regulate rail, road, and water carriers; establish Interstate Commerce Commission
1890	Sherman Antitrust Act	Prevent monopolies and cartels
1913	Federal Reserve Act	Regulate banks; establish Federal Reserve System
1914	Clayton Act	Strengthen antitrust enforcement
1914	Federal Trade Commission Act	Administer Clayton Act
1933	Securities Act	Regulate securities sold to public
1934	Federal Communications Act	Regulate radio, telephone, telegraph
1935	National Labor Relations Act	Regulate labor unions
1935	Federal Power Act	Regulate gas and electricity; establish Federal Power Commission
1936	Robinson-Patman Act	Regulate price discrimination
1938	Civil Aeronautics Act	Regulate civil aviation by Civil Aeronautics Board
1947	Taft-Hartley Act	Regulate labor unions

SOURCE: Arthur Johnson, *Corporate-Business Relations* (Westerville, Ohio: Merrill, 1965).

are listed. Each act, but one, is still in force; most have been expanded repeatedly since passage. Only the Civil Aeronautics Act, along with its regulatory program, has been phased out.

The Interstate Commerce Commission (ICC) and the Federal Communications Commission (FCC) regulate virtually every kind of interstate transportation and communication except airlines and newspapers. They regulate prices, entry, exit, routes, and services and financial and management practices of firms in the regulated industries. The Federal Power Commission regulates interstate transmission of gas and electricity. The Securities and Exchange Commission regulates financial securities sales to the public, financial reporting by corporations, and financial markets. The Federal Reserve Board, along with several other federal government agencies, regulates banks.

The Sherman Act, the Clayton Act, the Federal Trade Commission Act, and the Robinson-Patman Act are the nation's basic antitrust laws. They prohibit monopolies and monopoly agreements among firms and other organizations. In recent years, they have also been applied to local governments.

The National Labor Relations Act and the Taft-Hartley Act are the basic acts governing and regulating labor unions.

Table 11 contains an imposing list of regulatory programs. It covers many important industries of diverse characteristics. Provisions vary greatly from one program to another. Some acts contain detailed organizational, procedural, and substantive provisions. Others are brief and general. The prize for brevity goes to the Sherman Act, which simply outlaws monopolies and attempts to monopolize and provides civil and criminal penalties. The result is that the antitrust law has mostly been written by courts.

No particular set of economic attributes that might account for the government's decision to regulate characterizes many of the industries covered. Economists' concepts, such as natural monopoly, public goods production, or external diseconomies, played little or no role in federal government deliberations that led to the regulatory programs in Table 11. The only common characteristic of all the regulated industries and activities is that each was at some time the subject of great public controversy and all are represented in Washington, D.C., by large and well-financed lobbying organizations.

Post–World War II Regulation

Starting shortly after 1960, a large set of new regulatory programs was introduced.[2] In contrast with the prewar regulatory programs (mostly introduced during the 1930s) the majority of the new regulatory programs do not pertain to particular industries. Instead they regulate particular activities—polluting dischargers, pension plans, and so forth—that typically occur in many industries and economic sectors. Key legislation establishing important programs has been expanded and amended repeatedly since these programs were introduced (see Table 12).

The Food and Drug Administration (FDA) was started early in the twentieth century. Its jurisdiction was broadened dramatically during the 1930s. The 1962 Food and Drug amendments mandate pretesting of new drugs for safety and effectiveness and prohibit sale of products prior to approval by the FDA. The 1964 Civil Rights Act set up the Equal Employment Opportunity Commission to enforce the prohibitions against discrimination in employment contained in the law. The law and its amendments cover discrimination based on race, sex, age, religion, and national origin. The 1966 Traffic Safety Act mandates elaborate safety requirements for motor vehicles. The 1966 Mine Safety amend-

TABLE 12   POST–WORLD WAR II FEDERAL
            REGULATORY PROGRAMS

	Legislation	*Scope*
1962	Food and Drug amendments	Requires drug pretesting
1964	Civil Rights Act	Creates Equal Employment Opportunity Commission to prevent job discrimination
1966	Traffic Safety Act	Provides for safety standards for motor vehicles
1966	Coal Mine Safety amendments	Controls working conditions in mines
1968	Consumer Credit Protection Act	Requires disclosure of finance charge conditions
1969	National Environmental Policy Act	Requires environmental impact statements
1970	Clean Air Act amendments	Provides for air quality standards
1970	Occupational Safety and Health Act	Establishes safety and health standards for employees
1972	Consumer Product Safety Act	Establishes a commission to set product safety standards
1972	Federal Water Pollution Control Act	Provides for discharge and ambient water quality standards
1974	Employee Retirement Income Security Act	Regulates pension programs
1975	Energy Policy and Conservation Act	Provides for regulation of energy markets
1976	Toxic Substances Control Act	Regulates toxic chemicals
1977	Department of Energy Organization Act	Establishes department to regulate energy

SOURCE: Condensed from Murray Weidenbaum, *Business, Government and the Public* (Englewood Cliffs, N.J.: Prentice-Hall, 1981).

ments establish safety standards for mine workers. The 1968 Consumer Credit Protection Act sets complex requirements for disclosure of finance charge conditions for transactions involving credit. In 1969, 1970, 1972, and 1976, acts laid out the basic federal environmental protection program. Those and other acts and amendments impose direct controls on polluting discharges to air, water, and land. They are backed by regulations and key court cases whose volumes would fill several large rooms. The 1970 Occupational Safety and Health Act establishes safety and health standards for employees. Regulations are promulgated and enforced by the Occupational Safety and Health Administration. The 1972 Consumer Product Safety Act established the Consumer Product Safety Commission to set and enforce safety standards on consumer products. The 1974 Employee Retirement Income Security Act regulates pension programs of private profit-seeking and nonprofit employers.

The 1975 and 1977 energy acts provide for elaborate regulation of energy markets and established the Department of Energy to formulate and enforce regulations.

What characteristics does this group of regulatory programs have in common? First, and easiest, they all have goals that are desirable. Almost no one opposes their goals. The only issues are whether the programs do more good than harm and whether they are the most efficacious ways to achieve their goals. Second, the programs' legislative histories, the acts that establish them, and the regulatory institutions display a hostility toward profit-seeking corporations that typified the attitude evident in newspapers, magazines, and popular books during much of the 1960s and 1970s. Otherwise, it is difficult to discover what, if any, economic principles of public choice might lead to choice of the regulatory programs seen in Table 12. They are not unified by the likely presence of any market failures (discussed in Chapter 3) or by any coherent notion of equity (such as those discussed in Chapter 4). The irresistible conclusion is that these regulatory programs pertain to a set of problems that were of serious concern to a group of politically influential people and that they were passed because their goals are unquestionable and the political process was not opposed to additional regulatory programs. This idea is pursued in Chapter 9.

WELFARE ECONOMIC ANALYSIS

The regulatory programs just cataloged, and many others not listed, add up to an enormous set of controls on private economic activity. During little more than half a century, the United States has gone from only a few federal government regulatory programs concerned with a narrow range of problems to an enormous panoply of regulations of diverse activities intended to solve ill-defined problems and having vague purposes. The result is that almost no major decision can be taken in the private sector without consideration of its relationship to one or more regulatory programs. All institutions, profit-making and nonprofit, are affected. However, profit-making institutions are much more the subjects of regulation than nonprofit institutions.

Manufacturing firms, to take a broad spectrum of heavily regulated institutions, cannot make major decisions about new products, investments, prices, personnel policies, or financing without consulting federal agencies, reams of rules and regulations, court cases, lawyers, and accountants. Literally speaking, the federal government is a partner in every major decision in manufacturing corporations.

An army of 80,000 federal employees administers the federal programs.[3] An uncounted army of lawyers, accountants, engineers, and government relations experts is employed by private organizations and their Washington lobbyists to cope with regulatory programs. Most of the highly paid lawyers in private practice make their livings by helping private industry cope with regulatory programs, including tax regulations. Most federal courtroom time is probably given over to regulatory litigation.

It is almost unnecessary to ask whether the social benefits exceed the costs of federal regulatory programs. The analysis in Chapter 3 shows that these programs can accomplish little that could not be accomplished by private arrangements if the federal government simply laid down and enforced coherent rules governing property rights, with a small set of economic incentives built into laws to encourage and discourage activities that private arrangements cannot optimize. The prime candidates for economic incentives to alter private resources allocations probably are environmental protection and basic research.

Going down one layer of specificity, many economists have written books and articles about the social efficacy of programs cataloged earlier in this chapter. A substantial library of studies has been written about the pre–World War II industry regulations, and dozens of books and articles have been written about the more recent social regulatory programs. Much of this writing is by economists sympathetic to the goals of the regulatory programs they study. Yet the overwhelming majority of such studies are critical of the programs they analyze. Many studies fail to detect any favorable effects of the regulatory programs. Some conclude that regulatory agencies are unduly influenced by groups that are ostensibly the subjects of the regulations or by groups whose interest is in orienting programs so they are advantageous to influential groups but not to social efficiency.

Many scholars conclude that regulatory programs cannot meaningfully be said to be aimed at social efficiency at all but instead, are rightly viewed as intending to improve the welfare of specific groups. This conclusion implies evaluating regulatory programs as attempts to improve equity, not social efficiency. But the analysis in Chapter 4 showed that regulation of private resource allocation is a poor way to achieve equity goals. Perhaps more important, the groups assisted by most programs are probably not high on most people's priority lists of those in need of federal government assistance. Beyond doubt, trucking firms and workers benefit from ICC regulation, but what is the criterion for selecting them for assistance? Beyond doubt, many drivers benefited from price controls on gasoline during the 1970s, but why is that subset of the driving population an appropriate object of federal assistance? The desirability of federal regulatory programs must stand or fall on social efficiency grounds.

It is not possible to survey here the many economic studies of regulatory programs.[4] However, some brief discussions of a small sample of regulatory programs may help illustrate the preceding remarks. The following examples were by no means chosen randomly. But similar stories can be told about most federal government regulatory programs.

Interstate Commerce Commission

In a way, the oddest of the industry regulatory programs is the oldest. The ICC was created to regulate railroads, which were believed—and to some extent correctly in the nineteenth century—to be natural monopolies. As always happens with regulatory programs, it became apparent that, for regulation to be effective, competing transportation modes also had to be regulated. Thus trucking, pipelines, shipping, buses, and airlines came to be regulated. Since World War II, trucking has come to be the major competition of railroad freight transportation. No one who studies the industry thinks there is any significant element of natural monopoly in trucking. There are hundreds of trucking firms (and there would be many more in the absence of government controls on entry), and service can easily be shifted to routes on which profit is above competitive levels. For years, much railroad rolling stock has been owned by federal- or state-owned corporations, and rights-of-way are owned by railroad companies that appear to be in permanent bankruptcy or are fighting for their lives in competition with trucks and other carriers.

Thus the ICC has increasingly become an agency aimed at keeping freight and passenger rates high enough so railroads can survive. As frequently happens, an agency established to regulate an industry has ended up trying to protect it from competition. The goal can hardly be said to have been achieved. Many studies show that what has been achieved is to raise costs and prices and to slow down the adaptability, flexibility, and innovativeness of all regulated modes. Railroads are slowed or prevented from abandoning loss-making operations and from making needed innovations. Trucking is prevented from competing fully with railroads. No major change can be introduced without elaborate and time-consuming regulatory procedures.

No one has measured the loss of social efficiency from ICC regulation in the form of excessive shipping costs, delays in shipping, slow technical progress, and lack of variety and flexibility in modes, routes, and kinds of service.[5] During a century of excessive regulation, the loss of social efficiency must have been enormous. Almost everybody who has studied the situation agrees that ICC regulation is excessive. Modest reforms were passed in the early 1980s, and others have been discussed. The ICC serves no social purpose whatsoever; it should be abolished, not re-formed.

Consumer Product Safety

Many federal government agencies and programs regulate the design, advertising, sales, and use of consumer products.[6] One of the oldest and best known is the FDA, which regulates the introduction and contents of food and drug products for safety and efficacy. In addition, the Federal Trade Commission and the Agriculture Department administer consumer product regulatory programs. But the Consumer Product Safety Commission (CPSC) established by the 1972 Consumer Product Safety Act, has the broadest and most intrusive consumer product regulatory authority. The CPSC sets safety standards for a large but poorly defined set of consumer products, publishes warnings of product dangers it perceives, and can require recall and bans of dangerous products at the producer's expense.

Perhaps the greatest expansion of consumer product safety regulation in recent decades has been product liability imposed by courts. Some of the largest liability decisions have been handed down by state courts. During the 1970s, many courts developed a tendency to hold producers liable for almost any harm that resulted from almost any use or misuse of products.

Consumer product safety regulation can be criticized on many levels. The easiest criticism is that almost no careful studies have been able to find measurable benefits from any programs. Studies have not concluded that less harm has resulted from prescription drugs as a result of stringent FDA testing. They have concluded that the FDA is much more concerned that someone may die from a drug whose use it has approved than that someone may die because a valuable drug was not discovered or marketed as a result of FDA restrictions. Food and Drug Administration regulation has slowed introduction of new drugs. No careful study appears to have concluded that CPSC regulation has reduced injuries or deaths from consumer products.

The second easiest criticism is that there is ambiguity and overlap among various regulatory activities. The CPSC at one time thought it could regulate handguns for safety under its authority, despite the obvious overlap with state licensing activities. Much more important, courts hold producers liable for harm from products that have been approved for use by the FDA or CPSC. Direct regulation and product liability are obviously government programs and have similar goals of consumer protection. Yet no government agency has ever done a careful study of circumstances under which product liability is appropriate and circumstances under which direct regulation is appropriate. Nor has there been a study of the kind and extent of liability or regulation that best serves the public interest. Instead, agencies invariably attempt to increase the breadth and stringency of their regulatory powers, and their reports are partisan and self-serving.

Finally, the most difficult issue is whether any government consumer product safety regulation can conceivably improve social efficiency. Markets motivate design and production of safe and effective products by penalizing producers of dangerous or unreliable products. The knowledge that sale of dangerous products will jeopardize future sales of even their high-quality products motivates producers to avoid sales of dangerous products, even if consumers' market experience accumulates so slowly that the product in question would be profitable enough to justify the investments needed to produce them.

The most common contemporary argument for government product safety regulation concerns the ability of private incentives to generate and distribute desirable amounts and kinds of information on product characteristics. It was shown earlier that information has the characteristic of a public good. Many economists think that governments can approximate socially desirable production of public goods more closely than private institutions, but this general claim is false. For product characteristics in particular, competing and independent testing organizations can and do undertake testing and evaluation of a wide range of products. Undoubtedly, more of this would be done if government did not make it such a legally risky business as a result of laws that encourage suits against organizations that publish damaging information about products. Experience suggests that government is less willing than private groups to publish findings that may be controversial or may bring forth the wrath of producers. Even if one believes that government should produce information about products, that justifies only information production and not regulation.

Some economists believe that laws should hold producers liable for damages done by use of dangerous or defective products and that such laws would eliminate justification for direct regulation of product safety. The prior issue is whether markets provide adequate incentives for producers to assume socially justifiable liability in the absence of special laws for that purpose. Many products are, in fact, offered with particular guarantees, insurance, or indemnities. If consumers value such contractual arrangements enough to justify their provision, consumers are willing to pay their actuarial cost. Preferences by consumers for products with such arrangements make their provision by producers profitable.

Incentives for such contracts are limited by the difficulty in specifying uses of the product that are covered by the agreement and in ascertaining whether specific damage was caused by the product. A manufacturer of electric hair dryers might be motivated to insure buyers against the risk that the product might ignite the user's hair. Presumably, use of the dryer while standing in a bathtub with water in it would be exempt from the agreement. So would its use to defrost the refrigerator. But there might be an almost unlimited set of misuses, and it may be difficult to write a clear contract. Likewise, many prescription drugs have side effects that can also have other causes. Ascertaining whether a drug caused a malady may be impossible.

The temptation of governments, courts, and regulatory agencies is to overcompensate people in liability cases. A poor person badly injured by a product manufactured by a rich, impersonal corporation commands compassion from public officials, judges, and juries. The effect of overcompensation is to add unjustifiably to the costs of introducing and producing new products, thus motivating socially undesirable conservatism by producers. But consumers whose health or welfare is damaged because government or courts have discouraged discovery or production of a new product cannot sue and do not command compassion.

Theoretically, consumer product liability rules come under the heading of property rights as defined earlier. It seems clear that government rules should impose some liability on producers. For example, producers ought to be liable if they knowingly sell light bulbs that have a high probability of exploding when used in the normal way, and doctors ought to be liable if they knowingly prescribe treatment likely to worsen their patients' health. In general, producers should be liable if they do not divulge information they have about product hazards. They should also be expected to obtain and divulge such information if it can be done at costs that are smaller than the costs of likely harm to consumers due to their ignorance. Likewise, consumers should be liable for risks they assume with products if they know about such risks, or could have known about them at modest cost. It is unlikely that practical product liability rules can come close to a theoretically desirable rule. But careful legislation on the subject could induce more nearly optimum risk-taking by producers and consumers, reduce the amount of expensive litigation, speed innovations, reduce the confusion that surrounds the subject, and avoid the temptation to introduce wasteful direct regulation.

Congress has shown no interest in careful legislation on the subject of product liability. It is difficult to escape the conclusion that legislation and the recent trend of court cases on the subject are motivated by unquestioned desirability of the goal and by unthinking hostility to private business.

COSTS OF REGULATION

Four costs of regulation were identified: costs borne by the consumer and by the producer due to loss of consumer and producer surplus from resource misallocation, costs borne by government in formulating and enforcing regulations, and costs borne by businesses and other groups in complying with regulations. The net costs of regulatory programs are the sum of these four costs less any gains in consumer and producer surplus because of improved resource allocation resulting from the regulations. The preceding analysis and earlier studies of effects of regulation suggest that improved resource allocation from regulation is uncommon.[7]

It was suggested earlier that environmental protection might be one of the few areas in which regulation, or economic incentives, might be justified. Many studies have appeared in which benefits and costs of various environmental protection programs have been estimated.[8] Many such studies conclude that total benefits and costs of such programs are of similar magnitude. This implies that regulation is too stringent because marginal costs and benefits should be equated.[9] More important, the comparison is only of consumer and producer surplus changes that would result from efficiently run programs at standards contained in legislation. Every study of actual environmental improvement shows that improvements have been much less than government programs intended. The evidence is strong that environmental protection programs have caused much of the money the private sector has spent for that purpose to be wasted. In addition, such studies ignore enforcement and compliance costs as well as losses of social efficiency from reduced innovation and adaptability.

It would be a mammoth task to estimate the costs of all the many federal regulatory programs. The most ambitious attempt to do so is restricted to enforcement and compliance costs.[10] It concludes that such costs were $126.0 billion in 1980. That comes to $553 per capita or about 5 percent of GNP.

This estimate is substantial but is almost certainly far too low. Most importantly, it ignores the direct loss of consumer and producer surplus from federal regulatory programs. It would be surprising, indeed, if those costs were as small as the enforcement and compliance costs that were estimated. Finally, it is difficult to avoid the suspicion that the largest cost of regulation is the one that is most difficult to estimate: the loss of flexibility and adaptability and the reduced rate of innovation that regulation imposes on the private sector. Every regulatory program— whether food and drug programs, environmental protection, industry regulation, consumer product safety regulation, or whatever—demonstrably reduces the adaptability and innovativeness of the private sector. Every important change in product characteristics or of scale or location of production requires regulatory procedures and approvals. Frequently, approvals entail long delays and often require litigation. Increased delays due to recent increases in regulatory stringency have been estimated to be several years in the case of thermal electric plant construction. For the most part, however, regulatory delays are unmeasured. Perhaps the greatest harm resulting from the reduced growth rate of the private sector caused by federal regulation is the growing sense it causes among the population that the private sector is performing poorly. That causes people to be sympathetic to demands for even more regulation.

EXPLAINING REGULATION

The reason for the dramatic growth in the number and stringency of regulatory programs since 1960 is a mystery. There is no evidence that the private sector performed less well after World War II than in earlier decades; in fact, the evidence is that it performed better. Nor is there any reason to believe that there were substantial net benefits to be gained from increased regulation. No careful studies that preceded legislation had indicated a need for government intervention. Nor have careful studies shown that many regulatory programs have generated social benefits in excess of costs. It is difficult to believe that regulatory growth has resulted from a rational political process intended to improve social welfare.

One is almost driven to a political explanation of regulatory growth. Such an explanation must be that some groups are able to persuade government to use its coercive power to benefit them at the expense of average welfare. Such strategy was not discovered in 1960. For many decades, business and other groups have persuaded government to adopt programs for their benefit but at net social cost. In the United States, businesses persuaded government to benefit them by import controls, direct and indirect subsidies, such regulatory agencies as the ICC, and in many other ways; this started on a large scale about 1880.[11] What has happened during the twentieth century, and especially during the last half century, is that the power to influence government has spread to a much larger segment of the population. To a much greater extent during the nineteenth century than during the last 50 years, effective political power was concentrated in the hands of small elite groups. Although they induced governments to intervene on their behalf, by and large their interest was in small and unobtrusive governments.

As democracy has spread and a larger segment of the adult population has not only been enfranchised but also acquired the money and sophistication to manipulate government on its behalf, the result has been increased government intervention to further the special interests of a great variety of politically influential groups. The difficulty is that, with so many groups obtaining government intervention on their behalf, average productivity and living standards suffer.

At this point, this statement is a hypothesis. It will be developed and analyzed in Chapter 9.

SEVEN

The Burden of
State and Local
Government Regulation

The analysis of government regulation, which in Chapter 6 concerned federal government regulation, continues here, with a discussion of state and local government regulation. The conceptual model of the damage done by excessive regulation, developed in the previous chapter, is equally applicable here.

Economists have paid vastly more attention to federal than to state and local government regulation. For every scholarly book or paper on state and local government regulation, there are probably a hundred on federal government regulation. That ratio is certainly far greater than the proportion of regulatory activity or the likely harm done to the economy by federal relative to state and local government regulation. State and local government regulation has been a neglected stepchild of the economics profession.

One reason for economists' neglect is that federal government regulatory activities are much better documented than those of state and local governments. No document comparable to the *Federal Regulatory Directory* appears to exist for state and local governments. The closest, available only for states, are the *Book of the States* and the *National Directory of State Agencies, 1982–1983*.[1] These documents are apparently compiled for people who have business with state agencies, not for those who want to understand what they do. A second, and related, reason for neglect by economists of state and local government regulation is diversity. There are 50 state and about 80,000 local governments (defined as a governmental unit that has the legal power to tax and spend), of which nearly 40,000 are general purpose local governments. Different states undertake different regulatory activities, similar regulatory activities vary somewhat among states, administrative organizations vary among states, and regulatory activities performed by state governments in some states are performed by local governments in others. Thus compilation of meaningful data is difficult.

However, it should be noted that diversity also provides possibilities that economists have neglected to pursue—such as research to estimate damage done by excessive regulation. There is much more regulation in some states than others. Generally, states north of the Mason-Dixon line and east of the Mississippi River regulate more than southern, western plains, Rocky Mountain, and Pacific states. This provides opportunities for estimating effects of regulation at the state level. It is likely that excessive regulation is among the reasons that eastern and northern states have fared relatively poorly in terms of migration, unemployment, and economic growth since the early 1970s. Such research is less difficult among states than among countries because states differ less than countries and because inputs can move more freely among states than among countries.

State and local government regulation differs from federal government regulation for several reasons. First, the Constitution gives sovereignty over interstate commerce to the federal government and over intrastate commerce to state governments. Thus the activities that can be regulated by the two levels of government are theoretically different. This was an important constitutional issue in the nineteenth century, but in the twentieth century, the courts have permitted the federal government to regulate almost anything it has decided to regulate. For practical purposes, the distinction has become traditional rather than constitutional.

Second, states must compete with each other for businesses and jobs, much more than the federal government must compete with other countries. Thus state and, especially, local governments are more constrained in extracting and transferring surpluses from one group to another by regulation than the federal government.

Third, and by contrast, national elections are much better informed than state and local elections. The media provide much more information about the positions of candidates for national offices than about those of candidates for state and local offices. However, it will be claimed in Chapter 9 that most issues are decided by lobbying, not by elections. Actions of state and local government are less constrained by elections than those of the federal government. Interest-group representation

should be much more effective with state and, especially, local governments than with national. State and local government jurisdictions are
more homogeneous than the national jurisdiction and the number of
people that must be organized to be effective is smaller. This suggests that
one might expect more regulation intended to further interests of
particular groups at the state and local than at the national level.

Fourth, and finally, the federal government has grown relative to
state and local governments during the twentieth century. As was
claimed in an earlier chapter, regulation is endemic to government
spending. The implication of these two observations is that federal
government regulation may have become more burdensome than state
and local government regulation during recent decades.

The four contrasts just made are suggestive but not conclusive. In any
case, they go in different or ambiguous directions. The implication is that
the facts should be allowed to speak. A beginning at that task is made in
this chapter, but the following analysis will make little distinction
between state and local governments. Local governments are the
constitutional offspring of state governments. Constitutionally, local
governments do what state governments permit or mandate them to do.
Division of responsibilities between state and local governments varies
among states, but the division follows no apparent pattern.

A CATALOG OF STATE AND LOCAL
GOVERNMENT REGULATORY PROGRAMS

Most Americans have no idea how many regulatory
programs are administered by state and local governments. A sample of
programs that are of some importance and are found in more than a few
states is introduced here.[2] The purpose is not to provide a detailed
description or evaluation of regulatory activities but rather to indicate the
scope and flavor of activities.

Regulatory activities of state and local governments are divided into
three groups here: programs shared with the federal government, regulations of industries and related groups, and regulations of occupations.

Programs Shared with the Federal Government

Several important regulatory programs were established by the
federal government in laws that mandated state participation in the
program. In most cases, the reason for such division of responsibility is
that the subject had traditionally been a state responsibility. Because states

were not doing the job as the federal government wished, the federal government established a national regulatory program. Major responsibilities were left to state governments as a political compromise in a struggle between state and federal governments for program control. In no case is there evidence that the motive was efficiency. For example, if the details of an optimum regulatory program varied among states because of conditions that differed among them, it might justify leaving some aspects of the regulatory program to states. Alternatively, an entirely federal program with state offices that could tailor details of the program to state conditions might be appropriate. But most federal regulatory programs do not permit significant differences among parts of programs administered by states. Indeed, variation among states is disapproved of by federal and most state governments precisely because they fear that the result might be that states would compete with each other. That would be an ideal arrangement from the welfare economics standpoint (for example, states could tailor environmental standards according to citizens' wishes), but the positive theory of government in Chapter 9 indicates that governments are likely to oppose it because it would weaken their control over private activity.

All the important laws discussed in Chapter 6 are federal. The federal laws stipulate that states may administer programs provided they meet federal requirements. Federal courts have ruled that state laws may not contradict or, indeed, exceed federal rules. Thus the federal program permits little variation among states.

The prime example of sharing of regulatory functions is environmental protection. Federal laws require that the federal agency, the Environmental Protection Agency, administer state programs if state agencies fail to meet federal standards. The result has been enormous duplication and failure to coordinate between federal and state governments.[3] Businesses also are often forced to duplicate their efforts by obtaining state, then federal, approval. Theoretically, these are not independent evaluations, but additional time, cost, and inflexibility are imposed on businesses.

In addition, all states have an energy regulatory agency, which in part duplicates programs of the U.S. Department of Energy. Once again, courts have ruled that federal energy requirements take precedence over state requirements, but confusion has resulted.

Price and quantity controls over energy products, begun in the early 1970s, were gradually phased out, starting in the late 1970s and extending into the 1980s. Many remaining controls overlap with environmental controls and are administered by states. In many states, there are controls on locations, technology employed, and many other characteristics. Many states now have comprehensive state energy plans. Plans differ among states and have almost no economic foundation. No analysis has ever suggested why this form of state government intervention is justified or what it might accomplish. These plans seem to have been motivated by the anxiety about energy and the faddishness of government intervention in energy markets during the 1970s. Their potential for causing resource misallocation is great.

Other important state regulatory programs that are shared with or duplicated by federal programs concern consumer product safety, food and drugs, and occupational safety. In all these areas, federal agencies predominate. State programs duplicate, and sometimes extend, federal programs. To the extent that the state programs duplicate federal programs, there is no additional loss of consumer and producer surplus because of state programs. There is, however, an extra layer of enforcement and compliance costs. Two areas in which states go beyond federal programs are insurance and interest rate regulations. States regulate every aspect of insurance on homes, cars, health, life, and commercial properties, to name a few; this includes regulation of rates, entry, policy conditions, assets, liabilities, and the like. Consumer groups rarely demand insurance regulation or reform. Major lobbyists in state capitals are insurance companies and lawyers who make their livings litigating insurance issues. Interest rate ceilings pertain to home mortgages and to various kinds of consumer loans. They are normally set high enough so that, when market interest rates are high, high-income borrowers can qualify, but low-income borrowers cannot.

Industrial and Related Regulation

State and local governments regulate an enormous range of industries, a few of which have been mentioned before. Among those typically regulated are natural resources (water quality and quantity allocations, coastal zones, continental shelf, forestry, minerals, agriculture), housing (building and housing codes, land use controls, rent control, racial discrimination in housing, housing finance, insurance, real estate activities, energy conservation in houses, condominium conversion), education, transportation, public utilities, health (doctors, dentists, hospitals, home health care agencies, nursing homes, prescription drugs, pharmacies), banking and other financial institutions, tourism, alcohol sales and consumption, gambling, restaurants, funeral homes, and solid waste disposal.

In addition, states administer a variety of labor regulatory programs: minimum wages; hours and conditions of work; discrimination on the basis of race, age, sex, and the like; strikes; special labor requirements on contracts with state and local governments; child labor; employment agencies; and farm workers.

Not all these regulatory programs exist in all states, but all exist in many states. In addition, provisions of regulatory programs vary among states. It is also likely that one theory cannot explain all state and local industry regulation.

There are many documented examples of industries lobbying for their regulation by state governments. There are almost none in which consumer groups favored regulation. More impressive, almost no studies indicate any consumer benefits of industry regulation. States with stringent public utility regulation do not have lower gas and electricity rates than others. New Jersey, which has an ardent state insurance commission, has among the highest automobile insurance rates in the country. Stringent regulation induced several companies to leave the state, which induced still more stringent regulation because of the lack of competition. In many cases, one form of regulation breeds another. Rent control results in a large regulatory program to force landlords to provide services, such as keeping the heat up to 70 degrees in winter. Excess demand resulting from rent control eliminates the need for landlords to compete for tenants by providing adequate services, so laws are demanded to require landlords to provide services. Rent control also breeds regulation of conversion of rental apartments to condominiums, a procedure to escape regulation.

In some cases, the hands of interest groups are apparent. For example, construction unions lobbied for passage of state laws that require prevailing wages to be paid workers by construction firms working on state government contracts. Such provisions are similar to one in the federal Walsh-Healty Act, which mandates prevailing wages on federal contracts. Unions persuade government agencies to interpret *prevailing* as "union," thus curtailing competition on government contracts with nonunion contractors.

Occupational Regulation

Hundreds of occupations are regulated by state and local governments. Many skilled occupations are licensed: electricians, plumbers, taxi drivers, and chauffeurs, among many others. Many professional workers are licensed, typically by states: doctors, lawyers, pharmacists, landscape architects, teachers, nurses, and realtors, to name a few.[4] Sometimes governments also try to enforce minimum prices of services provided by licensed occupations. However, courts increasingly take the view that the result is a conspiracy between the government and the members of the involved occupations to fix prices and therefore a violation of federal and state antitrust laws.

The ostensible reason for occupational licensing is consumer protection: to protect consumers from unqualified or dishonest suppliers of services. Licensing agencies typically set minimum educational and training standards and minimum scores on examinations as requirements for licenses. Some require continuing education to keep licenses in effect.

Any occupational group has strong incentive to lobby for such regulation. Licensing laws typically contain "grandfather" clauses, which exempt those already practicing from the requirements. Then the educational and other requirements can be gradually strengthened, limiting entry and thus keeping remuneration high. Because consumers are equally endangered by existing and new unqualified practitioners, grandfather clauses clearly indicate the motivation for such regulation. Thus supply limitation is the key motivation of occupational members in lobbying for regulation.

Much occupational licensing is little more than a nuisance and probably does not cause substantially higher service costs. But no careful study has ever shown that licensing has a social benefit, let alone that its benefits exceed its costs. There appears to be no evidence that licensing improves the quality of services performed or that places with stringent licensing requirements have higher quality services than places with less stringent licensing requirements. It is invariably organized and licensed practitioners who lobby in favor of more, and against less, stringent licensing requirements.

The only conceivable justification for occupational licensing in welfare economics is the transaction cost of information. It is difficult and expensive for consumers to judge the qualifications of providers of some services. Thus it is argued, government should license qualified providers and exclude others from the occupation.

The basic argument against this justification has been made before: If private costs of acquiring relevant information exceed those of government acquisition, it justifies only information gathering and dissemination, not regulation or entry control. If it is cheaper for the government than for private groups to collect and disseminate information, then government can do just that. If examination and other qualifications are valuable to consumers, governments can provide them and grade practitioners who choose to participate according to this qualification. It would be no more difficult to ask an electrician to give proof of government qualification than to ask that electrician for proof of license. Of course, a private group might do the same thing. For example, an organization of practitioners could obtain and publish for consumers whatever list of qualifications it thought would be justified. If consumers thought the information was worth the cost, they would be willing to pay high enough prices for services provided by participating practitioners to cover the cost of providing the information. The idea of inquiring of tradespeople as to their government ratings probably strikes most people as bizarre. The reason is that people never think of licensing as being intended to protect them because, in fact, it provides them almost no protection. They rightly depend on their own experience and that of friends in choosing electricians and members of other trades. In this, their intuition is correct. Licensing provides no more than negligible protection to consumers. Protests of incompetence of a licensed individual to the licensing authority would be unproductive. A better remedy would be the courts. The reason undoubtedly is that most occupational licensing is to protect interests of practitioners, not those of consumers. Intuitively, most consumers probably understand the situation.

The same analysis holds for licensing of professionals. Nobody with sense thinks that the fact that lawyers are licensed protects them from incompetent or overpriced legal services. In addition, lawyers are self-regulated. If you think licensing is to protect consumers, not lawyers, take a complaint about a lawyer's malpractice to the state bar association. It is for good reason that people mostly take such complaints to the courts.

Medical doctors are the most emotional issue among licensed occupations. Not only are they the group whose qualifications are most difficult for consumers to judge but also the potential for harm from malpractice is greatest among doctors. In the 1980s, medical practice is deeply involved with a complex referral system. General practitioners or internists refer patients to surgeons, and so on. There is no reason to believe that the process should start with someone with nearly ten years of higher education. Many medical problems can be solved by practitioners who have less education and training. There is no reason not to bring in less qualified people at the bottom of the referral system. Those who oppose abolition of medical licensing ought to favor making it more flexible. As with other regulatory bodies, a primary function of medical regulatory agencies is to prevent such competition. Likewise, they oppose every proposal that would improve consumers' abilities to judge qualifications and related matters: advertising, posted fees, publication of data on success and failure rates, voluntary organizations to collect information about patient satisfaction, and others. Those facts are the best evidence as to whose interests medical regulatory bodies are out to protect.

SOME EXAMPLES OF
INEFFECTIVE REGULATION

Two examples illustrate the range of issues raised by state and local government regulation. The first is the most important and best studied regulation. The second illustrates the interest-group motivation of many regulations.

Housing and Land Use Controls

It is incredible that housing is among the most competitive, yet among the most heavily regulated, of all industries. Even in a local housing market, there are many consumers and many suppliers (owners of existing housing plus builders of new housing). None of the conventional arguments for government regulation applies more than peripherally to housing. It has no significant public-good aspects. Only minor characteristics of its exterior generate external effects, and studies show they have very limited spatial influence and are not very important.[5] Furthermore, they are least important in low density suburbs, where regulation is most stringent.

Yet housing is intensely regulated. Most communities have an enormous and complex set of land use controls that pertain to housing. Housing is also subject to housing and building codes, to environmental controls, to rent control, to condominium conversion controls, to a large set of landlord-tenant regulations, and to a range of controls regarding housing finance and insurance. Housing regulation is by far the most important regulatory activity carried out by local governments.

During the twentieth century, local governments have grown much less than state and federal governments. The positive theory of government discussed in Chapter 9 suggests that the reason for this is that local governments have less monopoly power than higher levels of government. With fragmented local governments typical in the United States, citizens can move from one local government's jurisdiction to another's without great cost and without changing jobs. The larger the local government jurisdiction, the more monopoly power the local government has, which helps account for the fact that spending and taxes are much larger relative to residents' incomes in large than in small local government jurisdictions.[6]

Thus local governments have little power to spend, tax, and regulate in ways that are contrary to the interests of voters. Voters can vote not only with their ballots and lobbying but also with their feet. But the need of local governments to reflect closely voters' interests implies that local governments pay little or no attention to nonresidents' interests. This intensely parochial character of local government has been the subject of a large literature, known as the Tiebout model.[7] The Tiebout model is about the interaction between spending, taxing, and housing regulation by local governments. It removes the mystery as to why housing is so heavily regulated and permits evaluation in welfare economics terms.

The model is easy to understand. Suppose there is a large set of nonoverlapping local government jurisdictions in a metropolitan area. Each local government produces a set of services available to all its residents and finances them with property taxes levied at the same rate on the market value of each dwelling in the jurisdiction. The local government services produced and the taxes needed to finance them are determined by majority vote in each jurisdiction. Then voters have incentive to sort themselves by jurisdiction so that, as nearly as possible, all voters in a given jurisdiction have the same demands for local government services and housing. Then, in each jurisdiction, voters are unanimous in favor of the desired set of local government services and taxes. Because all consume the same housing, all pay the same taxes, which are equal to the average cost per household of services provided by the local government.

Land use controls are a crucial part of the Tiebout world. Given the situation just described, a citizen with a low housing demand, perhaps because of low income, could move into a small house in a jurisdiction where other houses were large and expensive local government services were provided. The small house would be taxed at the same rate, but would pay only a fraction as much total tax, as other houses in the jurisdiction. Then the inhabitants of the small house would receive the same expensive local government services as other residents of the jurisdiction but would pay only part of the cost of the local government services received. Such a "free rider" can be exluded by land use controls, the basic purpose of which is to prevent dwellings from being built whose value would be less than the value of other dwellings in the jurisdiction.

The remarkable characteristic of the Tiebout world just described is that it is socially efficient.[8] Each resident consumes exactly the local government services demanded and pays the average (equals marginal) cost of their production. No person's or group of people's welfare can be improved (by moving to a different jurisdiction, for example) without impairing the welfare of others.

Of course, the Tiebout model is only an approximation to the U.S. organization of local governments. In practice, there cannot be enough local government jurisdictions in a metropolitan area to provide one for each combination of local government services and housing demanded. Only a handful of jurisdictions is typically available within commuting distance of metropolitan work places. They provide a rough classification by local government services, and their land use controls provide a rough classification of housing by jurisdiction but permit considerable variation within jurisdictions. In addition, some locational distortions are inevitable. Some people live farther from work than they otherwise would so they can reside in a jurisdiction that closely matches their public service and housing demand. From an explanatory viewpoint, both casual observation and careful studies suggest that U.S. metropolitan suburbs are extremely homogeneous with respect to both housing and income (the main determinant of demand for local government services).[9] Careful studies also indicate that the system is close to socially efficient, at least in suburbs.[10]

Objections to the Tiebout model are on equity grounds and start with the observation that it works fine for the 60 percent of metropolitan residents who live in suburbs. Since World War II, high-income residents have migrated to suburbs, where land is cheap and amenities are strong and where employment is increasingly located. There, they have formed jurisdictions with strong land use controls that effectively prevent low-income residents from leaving central cities. Central cities are too large and have too much diversity of income for the Tiebout hypothesis to work there. Until a low-income family in a central city reaches an income level at which it can afford suburban housing, increasing housing consumption as income rises results in higher local taxes but in no more local government services. Thus distortion results within central cities.

Closely related, but more important, the Tiebout world should be interpreted to be in violation of state and federal constitutions. State governments have permitted their suburban local government offspring to use their delegated powers to pass land use control laws that benefit some segments of the community (the high-income segments) at demonstrable cost to other segments (the low-income segments). Hundreds of lawsuits have claimed that the situation violates both equal protection of the laws and general provisions in both state and federal constitutions requiring that laws promote the general health and welfare of citizens. Only in New Jersey have such suits survived all appeals, and there they have had no discernible effect on local government behavior. Elsewhere, courts have accommodated their interpretations of constitutions to strongly perceived interests of the majority of metropolitan residents—and large majority of wealthy metropolitan residents. It is not a pretty picture in which courts and national and state legislatures permit high-income suburban residents to use the police power of their local governments to forbid low-income residents to live there.

Finally, land use controls are clumsy instruments of local governments. As has been seen, their basic purpose is to prevent dwellings whose taxes would not pay the costs of local government services consumed by their inhabitants. To avoid being declared unconstitutional, local governments must employ a long list of euphemistic requirements: minimum lot sizes, set-backs, minimum square footage, so many tennis courts per dwelling in apartment units, no more than 10 percent of apartments with more than two bedrooms (to keep out families with large numbers of school-age children), developers must donate streets, schools, and the like (to keep dwelling prices high).

As always with regulatory programs, land use controls cause long delays in construction, much litigation, locational distortions, and distortions in housing types (for example, too few multifamily housing units at prices that represent resource costs). Studies suggest that supply restrictions from land use controls have raised housing prices by 18 to 28 percent on the San Francisco Bay peninsula.[11] Although the San Francisco area has more stringent controls than most places, the controls analyzed in the aforementioned studies are not those that restrict total housing supply, but only those that raise costs per house built.

From a welfare economics point of view, all this is unnecessary. Other means of financing local governments would sever the link between house values and local taxes. Better yet, the conditions that make local governments socially efficient in the Tiebout model are those that also make private markets efficient. Most local government services— schools, swimming pools, health care, trash collection, and the like— could be provided as well by private organizations as by local governments.

An important reason that such services are provided by local governments is that local taxes are deductible on the federal personal income tax. Thus the costs of services are deductible if they are provided by local governments, whereas they are not if they are provided by a private supplier. In effect, the federal government pays for between 30 and 50 percent of the cost of local government services—through deductibility and aside from intergovernmental transfers—in high-income suburban communities. Of course, this is a misplaced incentive, not a resource saving. The fact that all local governments face similar incentives to overspend means that the resulting loss of federal tax revenues must be made up by higher federal tax rates. The result is to induce residents of high-income communities to vote and lobby for higher taxes and more spending than are needed for social efficiency. The effect is to strengthen incentives to employ stringent land use controls.

From the political point of view, the Tiebout world shows a politically powerful high-income majority employing the police power of government to the detriment of a poorer minority, which itself consists largely of racial minorities.

One of life's minor ironies is to see the same group of conscientious citizens at one local meeting to urge stringent land use controls on the local government to protect the character of the community and then at another meeting to urge the local government to lobby the federal government for low-income housing subsidies for the community because greedy landowners and builders make affordable housing impossible.

Land use controls must be among the most difficult kinds of excessive regulation to remove. They are to the advantage of a large and powerful majority, they reinforce and hide racial hostility, and they make use of devices that have long been permitted by state governments and courts. The place to start thinking about remedies is with the observation that, except for minor controls for sanitation and fire prevention, government controls on housing serve no purpose other than exclusion. Thus a state law or court ruling that forbade land use controls on housing would be ideal. Court rulings that local governments could place no restrictions on multifamily housing would be very useful. More likely would be rulings that communities must admit reasonable amounts of multifamily housing. That illustrates the strategy followed by the New Jersey Supreme Court, but because the usual array of controls is permitted, local governments can effectively exclude multifamily housing. Finally, removal of deductibility of state and local taxes on federal personal income tax returns would go far in the right direction.

Thus objections to the Tiebout model are more on equity than on social efficiency grounds. One can argue interminably about how much income should be transferred by governments from nonpoor to poor people. But elementary equity, as well as constitutional, considerations imply that the high-income majority should not use the police power to transfer well-being from low-income and racial minorities to themselves.

Taxi Regulation

Most local governments regulate taxis. Typically, in large cities, a commission appointed by the local government controls entry and sets fares. Typically, special licenses are required for drivers, ostensibly to set high standards for safe driving. Finally, vehicle inspections may be required, again for safety reasons.

Special requirements for safety purposes are probably not unreasonable, provided they are set at appropriate levels. In fact, there is not a shred of evidence that taxi drivers are more careful than other drivers or that taxis are safer than other vehicles. There is much anecdotal evidence to the contrary.

The justification for fare control rests on the justification for entry control. The term *entry control* is used here to mean prohibition of some potential taxis from entering the local business even though they are able to meet reasonable driver and vehicle safety conditions.

The only welfare economics argument for entry control is that it is justified to limit street congestion. In New York City, for example, cab owners use the argument that free entry would worsen congestion when they try to persuade the commission not to issue new taxi licenses, called *medallions*.[12] Despite the fact that city streets are congested, the argument is without welfare economic merit.

First, taxis are hardly used for commuting. Thus they are not typically on arteries during rush hours. Because most congestion is on arteries during rush hours, taxis contribute little to congestion. Second, given limitations on entry, licensed taxis congregate downtown where the most profitable business is. But that is also where congestion is worst. Permitting free entry would mostly increase taxi supply in outlying areas where congestion is less severe. Third, and most important, it makes no sense to limit one particular kind of vehicle on congested streets. Government policy in congested areas, such as Manhattan in New York City, should aim at making street use more expensive for all users (but only after improving the bus and subway systems). The result might well be to reduce private cars in Manhattan and to increase the demand for taxis.

In fact, supply restrictions on taxis are a perfect example of the way government regulation typically works. It works entirely in the interests of taxi owners and contrary to the public interest. It is an ideal subject for study because a free market exists for medallions in some cities, New York in particular, and their value facilitates welfare analysis.

There are about 12,000 medallion taxis in New York City; the number has been unchanged for decades. Medallions sold on the free market for about $50,000 each in 1984. Fares are set by a city commission. Demand for taxi rides is downward sloping, of unknown elasticity. The supply is undoubtedly highly elastic, except for restrictions on medallions. The supply of vehicles in New York is certainly highly elastic, and the industry employs only a small fraction of those qualified to do the work. Assuming, as a good approximation, that the supply is perfectly elastic, the effect of licensing limitations can be represented in Figure 1. The demand curve is D, and the supply curve would be S in the absence of entry control. The equilibrium price[13] would be p_E, and the equilibrium number of taxis would be T_E. Medallion restrictions limit the number of taxis to T_L, about 12,000.

The maximum price that can be charged with T_L taxis available is p_L. Whether the price is p_L depends on the regulatory agency. In fact, price is probably somewhat below p_L. There is more frequently excess demand for taxis in New York at regulated fares than in cities (specifically Washington, D.C.) where there are only weak or no entry restrictions. In addition, the interior condition of New York taxis is not only unpleasant but also dangerous because of exposed springs, and the like. If price were at p_L, taxis would need to compete for business and would offer safe, comfortable interiors, as they do in other cities.

Assume, as an approximation, that price is at p_L. The free market price of a medallion is $50,000. That is the capitalized value of the dif-

FIGURE 1   EFFECTS OF REGULATION ON
              TAXI SUPPLY AND DEMAND

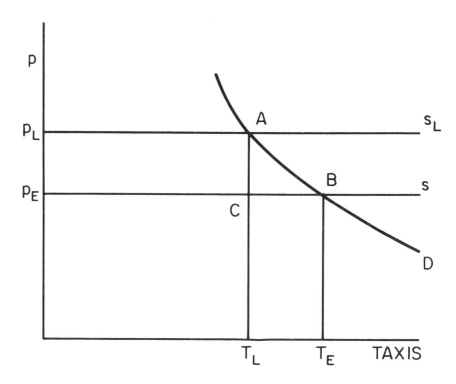

ference $p_L - p_E$. The higher the interest rate at which $p_L - p_E$ is capitalized, the greater the ratio of $p_L - p_E$ to $50,000. To be conservative, assume that excess prices are capitalized at 10 percent. Then $p_L - p_E$ is .10($50,000), or $5,000 per year. This means that revenues for a typical taxi are $5,000 more per year than they would be in the absence of entry restrictions.

The loss of consumer surplus from entry restriction is the area $p_L ABp_E$ in Figure 1. A transfer from consumers to medallion owners is $p_L ACp_E$, and ABC is the deadweight loss from government regulation. (In Figure 1, there is no loss of producer surplus, because supply is assumed to be perfectly elastic. *Deadweight loss* refers to the excess of consumer surplus loss over benefit to owners. It is simply the value to consumers of taxi services they are deprived of by regulation.) In this case $p_L ACp_E$ is ($5,000)(12,000) or $60 million per year. The size of ABC depends on the elasticity of demand for taxi rides. As an example, suppose there would be 20,000 taxis in New York if price were p_E and entry were unrestricted. Then ABC is about ½(5,000)(8,000) or $20 million per year.

These calculations imply that entry restrictions and excessive prices cost New York taxi riders about $80 million per year; $60 million is transferred to medallion owners, and $20 million is deadweight loss or waste.

The beneficiaries of the regulatory program are those who own taxis when the capital gains from entry control occur. Some of the real value of capital gains occurred years ago. In addition, real capital gains have occurred as demand has grown and the commission has permitted $p_L - p_E$ to grow. Many present owners paid high prices for medallions and would take capital losses if entry were permitted. That is an argument for removing restrictions slowly, say permitting medallions to increase 10 percent per year; it is not an argument for retaining the status quo.

Why does the political process permit government to regulate the New York taxi market so as to impose $80 million of unneeded annual costs on the taxi-riding public? New York's political process responds to the expressed interests of its 7 million residents. The $80 million loss to taxi riders is only about $11 per resident. Many New York taxi riders are nonresidents who have little political power in New York. Thus the loss per resident is probably somewhat less than $10 per year. This is a classical recipe for unwarranted regulation. A small group of taxi owners, probably no more than a few hundred, extracts $5,000 per year per taxi plus capital gains on medallions from a regulatory program that imposes costs of less than $10 per person on a large group of people. Thus taxi owner beneficiaries can afford to lobby and bribe to maintain the program, whereas those damaged do not find it worthwhile to take political action to prevent or rescind the program.

The preceding calculation pertained to loss of consumer surplus from New York taxi regulation. The other costs of regulation identified in Chapter 6 were administrative and compliance costs. Administrative costs are negligible in this program. Once the administrative agency is in place to license drivers and taxis, restriction on entry entails almost no additional cost. The major cost is policing black market cabs—people who have no medallions and thus have not made the $50,000 investment. That is a powerful inducement to illegal entry. Some years ago, illegal taxis (gypsies) threatened the entire regulatory program in New York, and the agency was forced to legalize some of the formerly illegal entrants. A major activity since then has been to prevent these entrants from competing forcefully with medallion taxis. The mechanism has been to permit gypsies only to answer calls, not to cruise. Compliance costs are negligible for taxi regulatory programs.

The remedy is obvious. Anyone who can meet reasonable driver qualifications and vehicle safety standards should be allowed to operate a taxi. If cities cannot resist setting fares, they should be allowed to set maximum, but not minimum, fares. Fares should be posted in clear, simple signs outside taxis, where customers can see them before entering. Competition would probably force taxi owners to post fares without legal requirements.

As invariably happens with occupational licenses, taxi regulation excludes relatively low-income workers. Permitting free entry in the taxi industry would provide jobs for low-income residents. A significant benefit of free entry, notable in Washington, D.C., is that there are many part-time drivers and taxis. In New York, owners cannot afford to keep their taxis off the street when customers are available. In Washington, many drivers moonlight, operating taxis at times of high demand to supplement income from other jobs.

CONCLUSIONS

Chapters 6 and 7 have outlined the kinds of regulatory programs administered by federal, state, and local governments. Catalogs of major programs have been supplemented by more detailed analysis of a small sample of programs.

Economists can, do, and should study and debate the theoretical merits of possible regulatory programs. But no economist can look hard at a sample of actual regulatory programs without concluding that nearly all do more harm than good. Few appear to have any social benefits whatsoever. Most either have benefits that fall far short of their costs or, like local government land use controls, have equity implications that are appalling. All regulatory programs reduce the economy's adaptability and flexibility, and all impair its ability to innovate.

EIGHT

The Burden of Government in Poor Countries

Most of this book has been explicitly about governments' roles in the United States and implicitly about governments' roles in high-income countries. Here the analysis focuses on poor countries.

Two notions motivate this discussion. First, poor countries illustrate dramatically and painfully the book's important ideas. Historical and cross-sectional information has been analyzed in earlier chapters, but it has all been drawn from a small set of countries that are now among the highest income countries in the world. Better tests of the book's hypotheses and better illustrations of its implications should be possible by broadening the comparisons to a larger set of countries representing greater diversity of political institutions and stages of development. Second, I believe the analysis developed earlier contains profound lessons about the prospects for growth and development in poor countries.

Each year, hundreds of books and scholarly papers are published about problems of economic growth and resource allocation in poor countries. The vast majority analyze some set of problems in one or more poor countries and governments' attempts to solve them. The vast majority of such publications conclude that governments have bungled the job but that the problems could be solved or alleviated if government intervention were more intelligent or better planned. I believe such publications are dramatically and disasterously wrong.

Just to establish that no straw man is being attacked in this chapter, reference is made to Gunnar Myrdal's monumental study, *Asian Drama.*[1] After an extraordinarily thorough study of the failures of government actions to promote economic development in Asia, the book proposes a wide and comprehensive range of government actions to develop and modernize Asian countries. It is the thesis of this chapter that the secret of economic development in Asia and elsewhere is for governments to do less, not more. There is no desire here to single out Myrdal's work for attack. It is among the best of literally thousands of books and articles written in the mode being challenged here. For every thousand scholarly publications urging governments to do something to further economic development in poor countries, it would be difficult to find one that urges governments to do less or even raises the question of the danger of excessive intervention.[2]

For the purposes of this chapter, the precise measures and criteria of poverty or lack of development are unimportant. According to the most careful scholarly comparisons available, some 40 percent of the world's population lives in countries in which average living standards are no more than about 10 or 15 percent of the U.S. average.[3] Avoiding such destitute poverty is the highest priority of human endeavor. Most parents would gladly work themselves to an early death to enable their children to avoid such poverty. Many people would cheat, steal, or even murder for the purpose. Many would, and do, sell their children to avoid destitute poverty for remaining family members. This is not the place to defend these assertions. However, anyone who believes that religion or philosophy dissuade people in poor countries from caring about poverty should look elsewhere for enlightenment regarding economic development.

Of course, some poor countries have much lower incomes than others. It is reasonable to define *destitute poverty* as living standards below about $250 per year per capita, in 1982 prices. That was about the average income in India. Using that standard, Latin America has pockets of destitute poverty, but most Latin American countries have living standards that are three times that level. Most destitute poverty is in South and Southeast Asia and in Africa. Bangladesh, India, Chad, Ethiopia, and Malawi contain much destitute poverty.

Why are there such enormous disparities in living standards? Beyond doubt, there are many reasons, having to do with history, geography, natural resources, and other matters. Nothing in this chapter is meant to suggest that inappropriate government actions are the sole or, in some cases, the most important explanation of economic backwardness. But the chapter is intended to make the case that governments are a major part of the problem.

GOVERNMENT ROLES IN
POOR COUNTRIES

In 1984, the World Bank tabulated basic data for 126 countries, of which 72 were classified as low income or lower middle income.[4] No country in these two categories had GNP per capita above $1,610 in 1982. That was about 12 percent of U.S. GNP per capita and represents average living standards no more than 15 or 20 percent as great as those in the United States. The 72 low-income and lower-middle-income countries contained 2.9 of the world's 4.5 billion people, about 65 percent of total world population. The 72 countries vary greatly as to geography, culture, and economic and political systems. Any generalization about them, except that they are poor, is certain to be misleading for at least some countries in the group. Nevertheless, some generalizations are presented here. It would take a long volume to describe, document, and qualify such statements; nevertheless, the 72 poor and near-poor countries differ in important ways from other countries and especially from high-income industrialized countries. I believe that some of the differences are important in understanding the poverty of these 72 countries.

Most Poor Countries Are Undemocratic

Basically, democracy is a system that compels government to pay attention to the interests of its citizens because citizens vote them out of office if they do not. The most undemocratic government must pay at least minimal attention to the interests of its citizens. Otherwise citizens may emigrate, revolt, or commit violence that is embarrassing or costly to the government. More specifically, even undemocratic governments must further the interests of at least some groups, such as the military and powerful landowners. In the most democratic countries, governments are constrained by free elections, constitutions, traditions, independent judiciaries, and other institutions to protect citizens' interests. It will be argued in the next chapter that even the most democratic governments protect citizens' economic interests only rather poorly. And some democracies protect citizens' interests poorly indeed. But nobody who has experienced both democratic and nondemocratic systems can doubt that differences in degrees found among contemporary countries are extremely important. Several publications attempt to quantify the bundle of restraints that political systems place on governments in various countries.[5]

Most poor countries have no tradition of free elections. In most poor countries, democracy is viewed—at least by governments and their supporters—as an alien, exotic, and dangerous concept. In many, there are no elections, or there are elections for only a restricted set of offices. In some, no opposition to the ruling party is permitted. In others, opposition is restricted within a narrow spectrum.

Of the 28 countries listed by the World Bank as having GNP per capita in excess of $5,000 in 1982, more than 25 regularly elect national and local governments. Of the 34 poorest countries listed, only 3 or 4 (most notably India) regularly elect national governments in elections with important opposition parties. Whatever the cause-and-effect relationship between democracy and economic development may be (the possibilities are discussed in Chapter 9), there is a moderately strong correlation between living standards and common measures of democracy.

Governments in Many Poor Countries Are Not Large

Several studies have concluded that even among relatively low-income countries there is a positive relationship between the share of government spending in GNP and GNP per capita.[6] But such studies do not adequately measure the importance of government spending in the economies of poor countries. They correlate general government spending per capita with GNP per capita. General government spending includes the typical budgetary categories presented in Chapter 2 but excludes spending by government-owned businesses. Many governments in poor countries are either communist or explicitly socialist. In either case, governments own most of the modern industrial sector, and its expenditures are excluded from government spending accounts. Until the early 1980s, private property of almost any kind was illegal in China. In India, there is much private property, but governments own much of the modern industrial sector and most modern utilities, such as energy and transportation businesses. Thus in these two countries, containing more than half the world's poor and near-poor population, general government spending vastly understates the importance of government spending in the economy. The Chinese publish no data on government spending or receipts. But the World Bank's estimate that Indian central government general spending was only 12 percent of Indian GNP in 1980 understates the economic role of the central government in the economy.[7]

The same is true, in greater or lesser degree, in most poor and near-poor countries.

It is nevertheless true that the share of government general spending in GNP rises with GNP per capita in poor countries. In most poor and near-poor countries, government general spending is 10 to 25 percent of GNP; it is typically 25 to 50 percent in high-income industrialized countries. That is hardly surprising. Most general government spending in high-income countries simply transfers resources, either in the form of transfers or goods and services, from politically less to more favored groups. A much larger share of GNP is available for such transfers in a rich than in a poor country, at least if transfers are not to impose an intolerable burden on groups who are net losers in the tax-transfer process.

Governments Have Excessive Controls in Poor Countries

The thesis of this chapter is that a vast array of government controls on economic activity is the key to understanding low living standards and slow growth in poor countries. Here the subject is discussed in a general way, following which a catalog of specific controls that are typical in poor countries is presented.

No one can study, or even be a perceptive traveler in, poor countries without being impressed with the overwhelming presence of government intervention and control in every facet of economic life. Unfortunately, the subject is difficult to document. No international organization classifies and catalogs government controls in poor countries. The subject seems to defy classification. For countries with a well-developed legal system, kinds of intervention can be ascertained. But many poor countries have poorly developed legal systems, and as will be seen, much intervention is informal and not covered by laws or written rules. Thus all the interventions discussed here can be illustrated for particular countries, but it is impossible to know how common they are or how they are interpreted and administered in many countries.

Many poor countries have communist or extreme socialist governments. In such countries, it is meaningless to discuss government intervention. Private property is illegal except for personal possessions and, in some cases, certain small businesses and perhaps some housing. Businesses, farms, and financial institutions are owned by the government, and workers are assigned to jobs. Such countries are not the subject of this discussion, which is restricted to countries in which important kinds of private property are permitted.

Within the set of countries in which governments permit private property, many have only poorly developed property rights. To take the best example, rights to land are poorly specified and complex in many poor countries.[8] In some places, tenure on farm land is governed by tradition and inheritance. Land titles may not be obtainable or freely tradeable even in urban areas. If land cannot be transferred with clear tenure, the result is to slow the process of changing land uses from agricultural to urban and other uses, which is a crucial aspect of economic development. Poorly defined property rights in land also add needless risks to investment in urban sectors. Ensuring that property rights in land are fully defined and transferable ought to be a primary responsibility of governments.

Property rights in man-made assets—structures and equipment—are better defined than those in land. But, of course, tenure in immovable man-made assets is no better than tenure in the land on which they sit.

For both land and man-made assets, there is inadequate protection against arbitrary and uncompensated seizures by governments. In most poor countries, governments can and do seize land for the flimsiest reason or for no public purpose, with little or no compensation. Mechanisms vary. Freezing prices several years before purchase by eminent domain is nearly the same as confiscation in a country with rapid inflation. Alternatively, other regulatory procedures can be brought to bear on owners who oppose property sales to governments on undesirable terms. Physical property is extremely vulnerable to coercive government measures. Absence of secure tenure to productive assets dramatically diminishes private investment incentives in many poor countries.

Governments in many poor countries also interfere in counterproductive ways with human resource allocation. Education is the most important kind of human capital accumulation, and it is almost entirely government owned in most poor countries. Many governments simply provide far too little education.[9] Many discourage private incentives for human capital formation—in education, training, and experience—by wage and price controls, excessive and arbitrary taxation, and controls on entry into occupations and industries.

A CATALOG OF GOVERNMENT CONTROLS

In the following discussion of specific controls that illustrate the ideas just introduced, attention is again restricted to poor countries in which significant amounts of private property are permitted by governments. Government control is a moot issue in a country in which there is no private sector to control. By no means all poor countries have all the controls cataloged here, but many countries have many of them.

Financial Controls

Most poor countries have poorly developed financial institutions: banks, mortgage institutions, stock and bond markets, and the like. To some extent, of course, poorly developed financial institutions result from the low levels of education and training that are endemic in low-income countries. Much more important is the fact that governments want to maintain control over financial institutions as a key means of economic control. In most low-income countries, governments own, or closely control, nearly all financial institutions.[10] Typically, governments are the most important source of funds for investment in modern industry.[11]

Much of the savings that governments allocate is invested in government-owned businesses. In many poor countries, governments own all or large shares of nearly all modern industry. Typically, rates of return in government-owned businesses are low.[12] Sometimes there is overinvestment, sometimes jobs are provided on a patronage basis, sometimes products are sold to politically favored customers at artificially low prices, and frequently government-owned businesses are simply run badly.

Being the main source of investment funds for the private or mixed sector gives governments great control over what, where, and how commodities are produced. Loans are typically made at below-market interest rates. Favorable rates are given for loans that will provide capital to produce commodities favored by government, that will produce in places (for example, away from large cities) favored by governments, that will produce by techniques approved by government, and perhaps, that will sell resulting commodities at prices and to customers favored by government.

Direct Controls on Private Production

In many low-income countries, private investment and production are subject to an enormous range of direct controls. In many countries, government permits are required for all except very small-scale production. Such permits may cover detailed specifications of inputs, outputs, and prices permitted to the firm. In India, given inputs a firm is permitted to buy or is allocated, it is illegal to produce more output than is specified by the permit.[13] Thus improved technology is illegal. India is far from the worst country in this and other ways. It is simply more democratic and open, and thus better documented. Despite Calcutta's terrible poverty problems, it is illegal to build or expand any manufacturing plant in the area because the government believes the metropolitan area is excessively large.

Price and wage controls are also common in low-income countries.[14] Keeping wages high and prices low generates support from favored groups without any government taxing or spending. The result is that private supply incentives are impaired. Excessively high wages are typically paid in government-owned businesses and frequently required in private modern industry. Perhaps the most damaging example of price controls is controls on rental housing. Rent controls pervade low-income countries.[15] In many countries, controlled rents are set so low that they do not cover costs of any rental housing except that for very high-income people, where controls are typically less stringent or not enforced. Then the government castigates the private sector for its unwillingness to supply housing to those most in need, and government becomes the major supplier of low- and moderate-income housing.

Another extremely harmful direct control is excessive city planning. City master plans are as common in low-income as in other countries, but they are much more harmful. They lack any economic foundation and cause extremely inefficient spatial arrangements in large, congested cities in poor countries. Specifically, they require excessive segregation of residential and business land uses, thus imposing excessive transportation time, costs, and energy use on urban residents. High-income residents and entrepreneurs can find at least somewhere to locate. Very low-income people—the millions of people who can afford only housing they build themselves with used or scrap materials—cannot. Typically, master plans make no provision whatsoever for self-built housing. The result is to force the poor to be squatters and therefore criminals. Because they have no tenure to land they occupy illegally, they lack incentive to make more than minimal investments in their housing. Their houses may be bulldozed the next day.

Controls on Foreign Trade

This subject is better documented than any other category of controls.[16] Many poor countries are highly protectionist. Typically, the goal is to protect government and private investments in modern manufacturing. Frequently, an agreement to control imports, and sometimes domestic entry, is part of an agreement with domestic or multinational firms to invest in modern manufacturing. Sometimes the infant-industry argument is used to justify such arrangements, and sometimes such domestic monopolies are simply passed out as political patronage or as bribes to government officials.

Many poor countries have domestic content legislation requiring products sold in the country to be partly fabricated there, and many have domestic ownership regulations requiring a stipulated domestic ownership, such as 51 percent, before foreign companies are permitted to invest and produce in the country.

International trade specialists debate whether foreign trade controls may be theoretically desirable in low-income countries. Almost nonexistent are careful studies that show that countries actually benefit from restrictions typically imposed. The strongest case that can be made is that, given the controls governments have imposed on locations, prices, wages, and the like, modern manufacturing plants would not be viable without an element of monopoly power conferred by import protection and other government actions. This illustrates again the proposition that one set of unjustifiable interventions leads to others.

Macroeconomic Policy

In Chapter 5, the harm done by inflationary U.S. government monetary and fiscal policies was discussed. The story, and the resulting harm, can be multiplied in poor countries. In the most inflationary years, inflation may be 25 to 200 percent per year in many poor countries.[17] As it is in high-income countries, inflation is unstable in low-income countries. Periodically, governments are seized with panic at the harm inflation does, and they crack down on monetary and fiscal policy. The frequent result is severe recession and sometimes political upheaval.

The motivation for inflationary policies is the same in low- as in high-income countries. Governments want to spend large sums of money on favorite projects and programs. Taxes are unpopular and difficult to collect. The strategy governments devise is deficit financing, which satisfies both goals for a while. In countries in which, because of excessive government controls and low incomes, there is little private savings to be tapped, deficits must be largely financed by money creation.[18]

The result of rapid growth of the money supply is rapid inflation. Inflation may start at a few percent per month but escalates rapidly. As prices rise, governments find that they must accelerate money supply growth, not only because it takes more money to have the same real effect but also because the economy performs more poorly as inflation accelerates and governments try to solve resulting problems with increased spending.

As inflation accelerates, economic performance inevitably deteriorates in both government and private organizations. Rapid inflation makes household and business budgeting almost impossible. Long-term plans and commitments are difficult or impossible. Households spend inordinate time and energy trying to protect their purchasing power between paydays. Businesses have similar problems.

Economic performance deteriorates even in countries where wages, interest rates, pensions, and contracts are indexed. Price comparisons become difficult for households and businesses. At moderate inflation rates, the details of indexing become major issues. If inflation is 100 percent per year, it makes a great difference whether wages and other agreements are indexed monthly, quarterly, semiannually, or annually. The situation is exacerbated because governments cannot resist using price and wage controls to curtail inflation. Black markets develop, and there are large and arbitrary redistributions of income and assets. Eventually, households and businesses abandon the currency in favor of barter or more stable foreign currencies. The former is clumsy and costly. The latter is difficult in many countries because governments fail to change exchange rates in line with inflation and inevitably introduce foreign exchange controls because of the resulting shortage of foreign exchange. Once again, one undesirable government action breeds another.

Eventually, governments realize the damage their actions are causing, or are replaced by other governments that understand, and clamp down. The readjustment from a situation in which inflationary expectations are built into every agreement is costly and painful.

Inflationary financing of deficits is discussed here as a control because, aside from the economic damage it does, it gives governments enormous power. An industrial loan at a 15 percent interest rate is enormously advantageous if inflation is 25 percent or is expected to be soon. Governments can have dramatic effects on income distribution by indexing wages to change quarterly instead of monthly if inflation is rapid. With 20 percent per month inflation, real income is 25 percent lower if wages are indexed quarterly instead of monthly. This is simply an indexing effect and takes no account of lost total output that results because rapid inflation impairs incentives.

Rapid inflation impairs production incentives and reduces the efficiency of all economic transactions. More important, it breeds instability. Perhaps most important, it induces both governments and private groups to expend socially wasteful efforts on protecting positions from inflation's ravages.

Informal and Unpredictable Controls

Perhaps the most important, and certainly the most insidious, aspect of government controls in many low-income countries is their uncertain nature. In many poor countries, governments have a wide range of powers to control economic activity, which they apply in more or less arbitrary fashion. Many poor countries lack an independent judiciary and a tradition of due process. Nondemocratic governments can change the laws and rules overnight. Frequently, it is unclear whether there will be reprisals if businesses do not do what is requested or suggested by government officials. In most poor countries, a requested action by a high government official is rejected at a business's peril. A request by a middle-level official, whose boss or boss's boss certainly has power to retaliate, may also be difficult to reject. If the middle-level official does have support from those up the line, rejection can be disastrous. It is frequently thought best to comply with almost any request by any government official, whether the request has a legal basis or not. In such situations, private investors are dependent on the good will of government officials. The situation inevitably deters private investment and can bring it to a halt. It is also a source of corruption, as business people bribe government officials or have money extorted from them in an effort to avoid adverse government actions.

It should be emphasized that similar problems are present in high-income countries. The greater and broader the powers of government, the worse informal controls are. Differences among countries are matters of degree, but such differences can be important.

WELFARE ANALYSIS

The thesis of this chapter has been that the most important threat to economic growth and social efficiency in many low-income mixed economies is not so much the size of government as measured by general expenditures or the burden of taxation, but instead, dramatic overregulation of the private sector by governments. Such overregulation inevitably slows growth and reduces the efficiency of resource allocation. In many countries, it has crippled the private economy. Simply put, the private sector does not work well in many poor countries because the government does not permit it to work well. Inevitably, the government blames failure of the private sector on greedy or corrupt domestic and foreign businesses and uses the argument to expand its spending and regulation.

It must be emphasized that the issue is not the profitability of existing private firms. In many cases, existing firms enjoy protected positions and are quite profitable. In some poor countries, private corporations are important supporters of the government. Instead, the issue is lack of competition, adaptability, free entry, innovativeness, and private investment.

Why do governments in poor countries engage in so much regulation? The welfare economics argument against regulation in poor countries is the same as the argument made against regulation in the United States: It can accomplish almost nothing that is socially beneficial and can do great harm. In many poor countries, excessive and arbitrary government regulations have crippled economic growth; in some, such regulation has brought growth to a standstill. The argument is made poignant by the following two claims.

First, the historical case for economic freedom is powerful. Suppose a government defines and protects private property rights with considerable scope; permits private businesses to invest, produce, enter and exit industries, compete, make profits, and go bankrupt; permits workers to choose jobs with considerable freedom; permits considerable amounts of imports and exports; permits private people and businesses to keep large parts of the returns to their efforts; and does not regulate private markets excessively. No government is perfect with any of these freedoms, but the approximation to them varies enormously by time and place. To take extreme cases, there is almost no trace of such economic freedoms in contemporary communist countries, whereas nineteenth-century England provided a good approximation.

During the last two centuries, no country in the world, regardless of its initial poverty level, has provided a good approximation to these economic freedoms for as short a time as two or three decades without resulting in rapid economic growth.[19] All presently highly industrialized countries in northern Europe and North America provided good approximations during the nineteenth and/or early twentieth centuries. Japan, Australia, and New Zealand provided good approximations in the late nineteenth and twentieth centuries. South Korea, Taiwan, Singapore, and Hong Kong have provided good approximations during most of the post–World War II period. All such countries have grown rapidly while economic freedoms lasted. The correlation between economic growth and economic freedom has been strong in Latin America during the postwar period. Furthermore, it is easier for presently poor countries to grow than it was for presently industrialized countries to grow a century or two ago. Much more usable technology is available from presently high-income countries for low-income countries to use (much of it free of charge) than was available for presently high-income countries one or two hundred years ago.

One can argue interminably about how close an approximation any country provides at a given time to the conditions listed. But the gross correlation between economic freedom and economic growth during the last two centuries is impressive and instructive.

Second, suppose that a government in a poor country rejects the historical argument. Suppose that, for ideological or other reasons, it insists on large government investments in modern industry, financial institutions, health care, education, transportation, and utilities. In most poor countries, these are the activities in which governments concentrate their involvement in direct production. Many of these activities can and should be financed by revenues from sale of products. Others, such as health services, can be financed partly by revenues from sale of services; other expenditures, such as public health programs, are not extremely expensive and yield high social returns. Thus such direct involvement in production normally does not require very high taxes; taxes equal to about 10 percent of GNP would finance such government activities in most poor countries.

Then suppose the government permitted the private sector to produce what, when, and where it wanted with only minimal government regulation and with adequate definition and protection of private property rights. Wherever the government thought the private sector could not do a good job, it could have government-owned production facilities. But government should not stop private groups from competing if they can. There could be no conceivable welfare economic argument for regulating the private sector or preventing it from competing regardless of whether there are also government-owned facilities. Free entry and exit, private financial markets, imports, and exports should be permitted.[20] If private firms attempted to monopolize, government-owned firms could undercut them without subsidy. No regulation would be needed.

The system described here would not yield the full benefits of private enterprise. If, as I expect, government-owned firms turned out to be much less efficient than private firms, scarce and valuable resources would be wasted. But the system could not have the stultifying effect on the private sector caused by the overregulation described earlier. Thus, if the analysis in this book is correct, considerable growth and improvement in living standards would result.

It is difficult to imagine that a government of a poor country would believe that permitting unfettered operation of the private sector alongside whatever government-owned businesses it chooses to have would slow economic growth. The stakes are enormous. In poor countries, what is at stake is whether millions of people (hundreds of millions in some countries) are able to live decent, comfortable, productive lives.

CONCLUSIONS

Why do governments in poor countries regulate private sectors so strongly when the social benefits appear to be patently vacuous? It is impossible to understand the magnitude of government intrusion into private-sector activities in poor countries within the context of welfare economics. Although governments may conceivably believe that the potential of monopoly or some other problem makes it undesirable to depend entirely on private businesses, that does not justify government actions that prohibit people from producing commodities to raise their living standards. Private production could be permitted freely alongside whatever production government wished to undertake.

I believe the key to understanding government regulatory and other actions in poor countries lies in the positive theory of government to be discussed in Chapter 9. That theory analyzes incentives that motivate government behavior instead of assuming, as welfare economists tend to do, that governments are interested in social efficiency and equity. The positive theory of government makes dramatically and painfully clear the reasons for excessive government regulation that have been outlined in this chapter.

NINE

Positive Theories of Government

Chapters 3 through 8 have been concerned mostly with normative issues, with what governments should and should not do to ensure social efficiency and equity. It has been indicated that governments are much larger and intrude more on businesses and on people than is necessary to ensure social efficiency and equity. This chapter turns to positive issues. Specifically, the question to be discussed is why governments are so much larger and more intrusive than they need be in order to do the things they should do in the interests of citizens.

This subject is important in two ways. First, identification of processes by which governments reach excessive size makes more plausible the claim made throughout this book that they are too large. To take an extreme example, if it were possible to show that government actions reflect strongly felt wishes of large majorities of citizens, it would imply either that citizens badly misperceived what governments can accomplish or that governments are not excessively large. Alternatively, if it were possible to show that governments grow almost regardless of citizens' wishes, it would add strong plausibility to the claim that they are excessively large. Thus identifying mechanisms by which government size and activities are determined is in part a test of the hypothesis that they are excessively large. Second, accepting the hypothesis that governments are too large, understanding why they are so large is a first step in reducing them to appropriate size. Understanding why governments are too large does not automatically lead to a means of harnessing them; it merely indicates where to look for methods of control. Similarly, understanding the biological mechanism by which cells become cancerous and multiply does not provide a means of preventing or curing cancer, but that understanding is crucial in knowing where to look for solutions.

Welfare economics is almost the exclusive preserve of economists. But positive theories of government pervade the social sciences. Historians, political scientists, and social philosophers have written about reasons for growth of government for many decades. In fact, economists are recent arrivals on the scene. Although there are wise remarks on the subject in earlier works, it was only after 1955 that economists began systematically to apply the tools of their trade to analysis of government size and growth. The birth of positive economic analysis of government can be dated either in 1957 with publication of Down's *Economic Theory of Democracy*[1] or in 1962 with Buchanan and Tullock's *Calculus of Consent.*[2] Since then, a large literature has emerged.

No one can possibly have read all the important literature on this subject in all the relevant disciplines. Nevertheless, it is crucial to place the subject in a broad context. Otherwise one risks attributing to narrow parochial causes phenomena that may be parts of larger patterns.

INTERNATIONAL AND
HISTORICAL PERSPECTIVE

Data presented in Chapter 2 indicate that growth in government spending as a share of GNP pervaded the industrialized and democratic countries of northern Europe and North America during the late nineteenth and twentieth centuries. Indeed, governments are both larger relative to GNP and more intrusive in northern European than in North American countries or in Japan. These trends suggest strongly that, whatever the causes of rapid growth of governments may be, phenomena and institutions that are peculiar to one country are not basic explanations. Some writers have been tempted to attribute rapid twentieth-century growth of U.S. governments to peculiarities of our governmental institutions, such as federalism or the congressional committee system. These national institutions may of course be parts of a complete explanation, but it would be dangerous to place great weight on them because they are not typical of countries that have experienced similar or greater governmental growth.

Most economists' research on growth of governments takes as its domain of discourse either twentieth-century governmental growth in northern Europe, North America, and Japan or some subset of this historical period and these countries.[3] But that domain is a very short period of world history and a small part of the world's contemporary population. The intent here is to place the positive analysis of government in a larger context in the hope that it will permit additional insights.

Basically, government consists of whatever group has a monopoly or near-monopoly on coercion. Inevitably, that correlates with whatever group has control over the most powerful weapons or military forces. Such groups have been easy to identify since the rise of the nation-state, four to five hundred years ago in Europe, more recently in most other places. During the twentieth century, it has been easy to identify sovereign governments almost everywhere, except during periods of struggle for sovereignty. Sovereignty has become institutionalized in well-defined government structures almost everywhere. Before the rise of the nation-state, however, it was not always so easy to identify sovereign governments. In medieval Europe, for example, a hierarchy of groups had limited sovereignty, mirrored in their rights to coerce and to exercise control over military forces.[4] However, in most times and places, it is possible to identify the group that has (or groups that share) sovereignty, provided enough records and other data are available.

Until two or three hundred years ago, it was characteristic almost everywhere—and to this day, it is characteristic in the majority of countries and in countries containing the majority of the world's population—that the primary government activity was and is extraction of surpluses from the predominantly agricultural population and use of such surpluses to benefit tiny groups of people in and near the government.[5] By *surpluses*, I mean the excess of production over that needed to enable the agricultural population to produce crops and reproduce themselves, commonly referred to as a *subsistence living standard.*

De facto and de jure political organization and the precise rights and obligations of rulers and ruled have varied enormously from one time and place to another. But the basic mechanism by which governments have extracted surpluses is quite simple and similar among most times and places.

Much evidence indicates that the competitive share of land in agriculture is 25 to 50 percent of total output. Competitive shares mean the proportions of total output that accrue to the owners of the various inputs (land, labor, produced capital, and such materials as seed) when input and output prices are set by competitive markets. In fact, agricultural production functions are such that input shares vary much less than relative input prices.[6] That land's share in total output is 25 to 50 percent is indicated by evidence about proportions of output or sales revenue paid to landlords as rent, by proportions going to landlords in sharecropping arrangements, and by direct econometric estimates of agricultural production functions.[7] Shares vary by crop and perhaps by technology employed, but fall mostly within the 25 to 50 percent range.

The basic implication of these facts is that whoever owns or controls agricultural land can easily obtain 25 to 50 percent of the income generated by farming activity. Farm workers are paid according to their productivity and can do no better elsewhere even if they are free to move. Given the ownership pattern, no exploitation of farm workers need occur. The element of exploitation results from the fact that its monopoly of coercion permits the government or its supporters to acquire rights to land rents by some combination of ownership or control. Returns that are generically land rents are extracted in the form of legal rents or taxes, but the precise legal arrangements are of secondary importance.

In fact, various devices have been employed historically to tie agricultural workers to particular plots of land. Devices range from slavery to serfdom to debt arrangements that prevent workers from leaving the farm and laws that simply prohibit job changes without government permission. The result is to reduce or eliminate the ability of agricultural laborers to move in search of higher earnings.[8] The combination of extraction of competitive land rents, artificial restraints on agricultural workers' wages, primitive technology, and natural population growth kept agricultural incomes at or near subsistence levels almost everywhere through most of recorded history, and to this day in many countries.

The point of relevance here is that extraction of competitive land rents is easy for governments. The land is immobile, and competitive rents are easy to collect with a minimum of coercion. Government needs only to protect the land from seizure and to turn away the farmer who does not pay the rent or taxes. Government need not even have legal title to land, although legal title usually rests either with government or with landlords who are closely associated with government and who convey to the government part of the rents they collect. It is much more difficult to control workers' movements (at least in the long run), but it is of secondary importance.

These prosaic facts are the key to understanding the support base of all the world's great empires, estates, plantations, magnificent palaces, country houses, and cathedrals until the beginnings of industrialization and large-scale trade three or four hundred years ago. Agricultural land was virtually the only form of income-producing property, and ownership or control of large amounts of agricultural land were virtually the only ways to achieve great wealth. Thus extraction of competitive rents through ownership or taxation of agricultural land was the primary goal of governments. To this day, it remains the pattern in large parts of the world. Scattered historical evidence suggests that governments were able to extract 25 to 50 percent of total output from the economy throughout most of history, as this analysis of competitive agricultural land rents suggests is possible.[9]

Of course, no government has absolute coercive power. Throughout most of history and most of the world, only a tiny part of the population received significant benefits from rents and taxes that governments collected. Beneficiaries have always included the ruler, the court, and those in charge of military forces and might include a few large landowners who might stand in any of several relationships to the ruler. In addition, some services are typically provided that benefit agricultural workers, large numbers of whom might otherwise leave or revolt. The most frequently identified service is military protection. However, to the extent that the agricultural population was about as well off under one ruler as another, the military should be thought of as protecting the government's taxes and rents, not the farm population. Most military action was to establish the ability to collect rents and taxes.

Beginning about five hundred years ago, people began to gain some control over their governments in a few places in northern Europe, notably England.[10] Slowly and painfully, people in a few countries began to restrain governments from extracting such large surpluses. The concept of private property emerged, and the notion grew that people had rights to income from their earnings and property. Closely related is the notion that people have a right to security from arbitrary seizure of and interference with not only their property but also their persons. Growing restraint on government correlated closely with growth of democracy and the industrial revolution. Restraint of governments relates naturally to the notion that governments should further the interests of the people and that the people should dismiss the government when they felt it did not serve their interests.

The relationship between growth of democratic restraints on government and the industrial revolution is more complex. Certainly, the growing restraint of government unleashed the productive energies of people. The fact that their property was more secure and that they could retain for their use a large part of their earnings from production inspired investment, savings, trade, innovation, and hard work.

The reverse causation must also have been important. Whereas governments were accustomed to extracting surpluses mainly from agriculture, industrialization created centers of power and wealth other than those based on agriculture. Industrialists and traders stood to benefit greatly from government restraint and the market dominance that government restraint permitted. In addition, although industrialization generated assets, earnings, and profits that were tempting for governments to extract, extraction of these surpluses was much more difficult than extraction of agricultural surpluses. Once industrial capital is in place, it is vulnerable to government seizure of the assets or the resulting incomes. But in the long run, produced capital can be moved to countries where governments provide a hospitable environment for business. This international mobility limited governments' ability to extract surpluses from industrial activity and stands in contrast with agriculture. Once industrial power centers were established, they provided an effective political force to restrain governments. Finally, during the eighteenth and nineteenth centuries, not only capital but also labor became internationally mobile in northern Europe. Both labor and capital left countries with unrestrained governments.

This is by no means an adequate account of the rise of industry and democracy in northern Europe, North America, and a few other places during the last two or three centuries. Four or five centuries ago, governments appeared to be in as complete control in Europe as they were elsewhere. Historians have not yet provided a coherent account of the reasons governments lost control in some places. Indeed, it may be that the reasons vary somewhat from one time and country to another. It may be that, whatever the reasons, the restraint of government unleashed a flood of energy, investment, and innovation that produced the industrial revolution. Once unleashed, the pattern would be likely to spread to nearby countries that were economically competitive and culturally similar.[11] Whatever combination of improved education, technology, and democratic ideology inspired by writings of social philosophers or the dynamics of industrialization may have caused the industrial revolution and the correlated growth of democracy and government restraint, the result was profound. Not only were social and political arrangements changed to the benefit of the vast majority of the governed, but also living standards of average people rose significantly above subsistence levels for the first time in human history. Whether it is one among several causes or the primary cause of the rise of democracy, industrialization is certainly a threat to nondemocratic governments. The threat must be a major reason for the ambiguous attitude that governments in third-world countries have toward the processes of urbanization and industrialization. Presumably, it also accounts for attempts by third-world governments to keep control of everything, as discussed in Chapter 8.

In most presently industrialized and democratic countries, government restraint reached its apogee late in the nineteenth century. Since then, as shown in Chapter 2, governments have grown and become increasingly intrusive. The purpose of this excursion into stylized economic and political history is to suggest that understanding twentieth-century growth of governments may require that one start with evidence from earlier centuries. The century or two preceding the twentieth constituted a period of increasing government restraint in what are today's industrialized democracies. That trend has been reversed during the last hundred years or so. What is the difference? What differences account for the dramatic differences in trends between the two periods? The disturbing possibility suggests itself that the century or two of government restraint was a mere historical aberration that existed while governments learned to control and to extract large surpluses from industrialized and monetized economies. Such a process would inevitably be slow, not only because major political changes are always slow but also because the international mobility of capital and labor in industrialized countries prevents one national government from getting far ahead of others in surplus extraction.

CONCEPTUAL BACKGROUND TO
POSITIVE THEORIES OF GOVERNMENT

Positive theories of government have certain conceptual elements that provide a framework within which specific theories will be considered.

The preceding discussion suggests what economic theory compels: that the right way to think about government behavior is to assume that people in government have the same motivations as everyone else. Economists have long assumed that people in the private sector behave so as to make themselves as well off as possible. Firm and other asset owners try to obtain the largest possible long-run returns on their assets. Households make employment and consumption decisions so as to make their well-being or utility levels as great as possible. It could hardly be otherwise than that people in government are similarly motivated. The constraints and opportunities are different, but not the motivation.

This simple assumption, which hardly seems disputable, makes much of history intelligible. It implies that governments extract from economies under their jurisdiction as much surplus or output as possible and use the surplus to benefit the smallest group possible. Every political system places some constraints on governments' power to extract surpluses. Most historical and contemporary political systems impose only mild constraints on this power. Although institutional details vary enormously, the foregoing seems to be a good approximation to what governments have done throughout history in nondemocratic countries.[12]

Although this simple motivational assumption provides important insights, it is inadequate at the next level of detail. Governments consist of different people with different interests and constraints. Some firms also consist of large numbers of people with varied interests. When markets are competitive, firms are inexorably driven to maximize profits; otherwise they disappear by bankruptcy, buy-out, or merger. No such simple mechanism controls governments' behavior. Governments do compete with each other. Competition among national governments for workers and capital was mentioned earlier, but such competition has undoubtedly become less important during the last century or so as governments have learned to control international movements of people and capital. In addition, sovereign state governments compete with each other within the United States, and that undoubtedly helps limit their ability to extract surpluses. But competition cannot provide adequate protection from sovereign governments. In the twentieth century, they can and do control emigration and export of capital, thus limiting competition among countries for people and capital. Sovereign governments cannot literally or legally go bankrupt, and they cannot be bought out by others able to run them better. Thus the concept of competition is of little help in making the motivations of governments more precise or in extracting implications about behavior from motivational assumptions.

At the most detailed level, different groups have different interests within any government. What benefits one department may harm another. In the U.S. government, Congress has interests different from the president's. However, for purposes of this book, it may be sufficient to identify certain variables about which specific assumptions can be made.

First, almost everyone in a policy-making position in almost any government benefits from a large government. At every policy-making layer, the larger the government, the greater are salaries and power. The foregoing is true regardless of whether size is measured by number of employees or by money available to spend in the private sector, whether it be spent on dams, transfers, or missiles.

Second, almost everyone in a policy-making position benefits from a large element of control over the private sector. Control over private activities correlates with size, salaries, and the power of both elected and appointed officials who are deferred to by controlled groups, who find employment opportunities outside government, and who have opportunities for bribes, extortion, campaign contributions, and related benefits. The kinds of benefits available depend greatly on the nature of the government and of its controls over the private sector. But benefits to government officials correlate with power over the private sector in almost any conceivable kind of government.

Third, most people in policy-making positions benefit from being responsible to as few people in the private sector as possible. The need to answer to large numbers of citizens limits the power and discretion of government officials.

These three assumptions merely assert that government size, the extent of government control, and the extent of accountability affect the well-being of almost all those in any government who are in positions to influence the size and activities of the government. Size and extent of control contribute to the well-being of government officials; accountability to the governed detracts from officials' well-being.

These three assumptions hardly paint government officials as ogres. Similar assumptions could be, and are, made about people's motivations in the private sector. The three assumptions clearly imply that, unless restrained by democratic processes, governments are larger and more intrusive than is in the interests of the governed. Positive theories of government differ somewhat as to the motives they ascribe to governments, but they differ most profoundly as to the nature of the constraints they assume that democracy imposes on governments.

Democracy constrains the extraction and use of surpluses by governments. In a democratic country, the electorate can dismiss a government that ignores the electorate's interests. How closely various forms of democracy constrain governments is a matter for analysis and speculation.

Industrialized countries have become more democratic during the last two or three centuries. National elections have been introduced, franchises have been repeatedly expanded, and the information available to the governed about government activities has increased. This has two strong implications for theories intended to explain growth of goverernments during the twentieth century. First, it would be dangerous to assume that governments have grown against the strong wishes of a large majority of the electorate. Such an assumption would make it difficult to explain why the apparently increasing control of citizens over governments has been ineffective. Second, whatever the other implications of the growth of the franchise and other means of access to political power in democracies, one implication has been to increase the number of people who must benefit from government actions. Twentieth-century democratic governments cannot remain in power without spreading benefits from their activities widely. In the United States, which is probably an extreme case, even groups that are a tiny percent of the electorate can extract benefits from government if they are well organized and well financed. Benefits may include payments in the form of transfers to, and purchases of goods and services from, favored groups; provision of goods and services to them; tax concessions; and regulatory controls that improve the groups' market positions.

POSITIVE THEORIES TO EXPLAIN
THE GROWTH OF GOVERNMENTS

Important approaches to explaining the twentieth century growth of governments are surveyed here. A classification of approaches is proposed, and prominent examples of research under each heading are outlined. No attempt is made to survey all significant contributions, which would be difficult or impossible with such a scattered literature.

All of the contributions considered take as their domain the growth of governments in the twentieth century. None attempts an explanation that would encompass both the decline in the roles of at least a few governments during the preceding two or three centuries and their growth during the present century. It was suggested earlier that restriction to twentieth-century growth may obscure key pieces of the puzzle. However, the difficulty of the subject and the scarcity of useable national income statistics prior to the last century have daunted scholars. A further restriction on the domain of discussion is that it is limited to high-income, industrialized, and democratic countries. This restriction is motivated by the fact that it is in that set of countries in which dramatic growth of governments has been observed. And all the approaches surveyed here assume that governments are constrained in important ways by democratic processes.

It was noted earlier that governments, like firms, households, and other institutions, maximize their control over resources. Governments' control over resources is greater the greater their spending, the more control they have over the private economy, and the less they are accountable to the citizenry.

Firms and households are limited in their efforts to control resources by competition from actual or potential institutions that are similar. Governments are limited mainly by a political process. Ideally, competition induces firms and households to behave so as to place the economy on the utility frontier, even though each institution is motivated by parochial concerns. Similarly, an ideal democratic process would constrain governments to behave so as to place the economy at an equitable point on the utility frontier, even though governments' motivations are parochial. The positive theory of government is about the efficacy of constraints imposed by democratic processes on governments' behavior.

The point of this book has been that governments in the United States and elsewhere are excessively large and intrusive in comparison with welfare economics goals of social efficiency and equity. But before surveying theories of excessive government size, it is worthwhile to survey briefly attempts to estimate how much too big governments are.

Most work on this subject stems from a provocative paper by Baumol, whose idea is that supply and demand for government services are much like supply and demand for private services.[13] On the supply side, the salient characteristic is that service production is labor intensive. This implies that, as labor costs have risen relative to capital costs in the twentieth century, service prices have risen relative to product prices. Furthermore, much technical progress is related to improvements in capital equipment, so technical progress is likely to be faster in product than in service production. On the demand side, service demands have high-income elasticities. Per capita demands for education, health care, and many other government and private services have risen rapidly as incomes have risen during recent decades. This combination of demand and supply characteristics makes it unsurprising to Baumol and others that budget shares of spending on both government and private services have risen.

Several scholars have tried to estimate the effects of these supply and demand characteristics on growth of U.S. governments during the twentieth century. In the most careful and comprehensive study, Borcherding estimates that slow technical progress and high income and low price elasticities of demand explain about half the growth in real per capita U.S. government spending during the first seven decades of the century.[14]

Although such estimates leave half the per capita growth of governments to be explained by noneconomic considerations, they take as given several factors that ought to be questioned. First, they take as given the estimates that technical change in government service provision has been only half that in private service provision.[15] Explanation of that fact may be important in understanding government growth. It is one thing if there happens to have been less technical progress in services that governments produce than in those privately produced. But it is another thing if the political process inhibits innovation compared with the private sector. Second, they accept as given estimates of the income elasticity of demand derived from data on consumptions of private services. Those estimates are invariably large. As was shown in Chapter 3, government services should not be similar to private services. Among the few justifications for government provision of services would be that the services had important characteristics of certain public goods. But a key characteristic of a public good is that costs do not rise as more people consume the service. Costs may rise somewhat as the quality of government-provided public goods increases, but costs should rise considerably less rapidly than income per capita. In any case, there is little evidence of increases in the quality of government-provided services in the United States. In fact, services such as mail delivery, elementary and secondary education, and police protection provide strong evidence to the contrary. Third, these estimates take as given the set of services provided by governments, whereas in recent years, governments have provided many services that they did not provide in the early decades of the century. Government expansion has not been mainly a matter of increased provision of services (such as education and police protection) that governments have provided throughout the last century. Instead, expansion has entailed the assumption by governments of a wide range of functions that they had not formerly performed. That might be accounted for by the assumption, for which there is no evidence, that income elasticities of demand for government-provided services are low at low-income levels and rise at high-income levels. But as was shown in Chapters 6 and 7, it cannot be accounted for by a finding of high income elasticities of demand. Likewise, nearly all government regulatory programs are functions they have assumed during the last century and not expansions of earlier programs. Fourth, as service prices become high in the private sector, products are substituted for services. For example, as domestic help has become expensive, washing machines and vacuum cleaners have been substituted. Yet as government services have become expensive, government has increased the number and kinds of services it provides.

Thus analysis of general supply and demand characteristics of service industries seems to explain only a small part of twentieth-century growth of governments. It seems that more specific analysis is needed. There is a strong presumption that the key to understanding the massive twentieth-century growth of governments lies in specifically political phenomena. Somehow, democratic decision-making and resource allocation procedures have led to growth of governments that defies understanding in purely economic terms. I turn now to analyses of that process.

A substantial group of scholars has analyzed how private interests of citizens can result in excessive activity in governments. Although theories differ from each other, differences tend to be in emphasis, not in basic issues. In fact, most theories surveyed here are not mutually contradictory. There is no strong presumption that only one mechanism is at work to cause excessively large governments. All or several theories may be correct or partly correct.

Several theories are based on differences between the ways benefits and costs of many things governments do or might do are distributed among the population. Consider actions that governments might take that would confer large per capita benefits on a small minority of the population whereas the costs of the actions are small per capita and imposed on a large part or all of the population. Many expenditure programs financed from taxes levied on all or most of the population have this property. Significant agricultural subsidies are paid to farmers who constitute less than 2 percent of the voting population—benefits per recipient are large for a small minority of people. Such subsidies are financed from general federal government revenues raised by taxes that are levied on a large majority of the population and are therefore small per capita. Federal and state subsidies to higher education have the same characteristics; so do federal housing subsidies and many other government spending programs.

Government actions that provide large per capita benefits to small groups at the expense of small per capita costs to much larger groups are by no means limited to expenditure and tax programs. The same is true of many regulatory programs. States license many occupations, with the effect of restricting supplies of goods and services produced. The result is to raise the incomes of those favored with licenses and to raise prices for consumers of the goods and services produced. Once again, benefits are large per capita for a small minority of voters, and costs are small per capita for a large minority or majority of voters. Federal programs control entry into many industries with the same effects. Tariffs, quotas, and other controls on imports from abroad have similar effects.

Theories based on concentrated benefits and dispersed costs can be referred to as interest group theories of excessive government size. Leading contributors to such analysis include Buchanan and Tullock, Friedman and Friedman, Stigler, Peltzman, and Demsetz.[16]

How can interest-group theories explain excessive sizes of governments? Why does the democratic process not prevent government actions whose total benefits fall short of total costs?

The easy answer comes from the system of majority voting in democracies. Consider a government spending proposal to be financed by taxes levied equally on the entire population. If 51 percent of the population will obtain benefits from the proposal in excess of the taxes they will pay to finance it, their legislators can pass the proposal by a bare majority even though total benefits and benefits to the 49 percent minority are less than the taxes needed to finance the program. Exactly the same analysis applies to an analogous regulatory program.

Note that the earlier assumptions about governments' motivations reinforce these conclusions. Elected and appointed government officials are likely to prefer programs that enlarge government spending and control, so they will try to persuade people to favor or not oppose such programs. It is clear that government officials have at least some power over constituents' views on such issues and that they frequently use that power to enlarge government.

In practice, the situation is worse than is suggested by this analysis. The proposed government action that commands a 51 percent majority may be a set of proposals instead of a single proposal. To be specific, suppose that a government can undertake several spending programs, each of which is worth \$1.00 to 11 people in a population of 100 people. Each program benefits a disjoint set of 11 people. Each program costs \$15.00 and, if adopted, is financed by a tax of \$0.15 levied evenly on all 100 people. Thus each program has total benefits equal to \$11.00 and total costs equal to \$15.00, so no program passes the overall benefit-cost principle. Each moves the economy off the utility frontier. Each, however, has benefits that exceed its costs to 11 percent of the population. The net benefit to each program beneficiacy is \$0.85 (\$1.00 − \$0.15). Legislators representing five such interest groups can get together, and each can agree to vote for all five programs if the others do the same. The result is five such programs passed by a majority vote of legislators representing 55 percent of the voters. The characteristics of the package of five programs can be summarized as follows:

Total benefits:	$5 \times 11 \times \$1.00 =$	\$55.00
Total costs:	$5 \times \$15 =$	\$75.00
Net benefits to 55 beneficiaries:	$55 (\$1.00 - \$.75) =$	\$13.75
Net benefits to 45 nonbeneficiaries:	$45(-\$.75) =$	$-\$33.75$
Net social benefits:	$\$13.75 - \$33.75 =$	$-\$20.00$

In the United States, this process (which also exists in other countries) is referred to as *logrolling*. *Logrolling* means an agreement among a set of legislators to provide mutual support for a set of proposals that together command a majority vote even though none of the proposals separately commands a majority. A better name might be *coalition formation*. It has been analyzed by Buchanan and Tullock and by Tullock.[17] Logrolling is exacerbated by the committee system of the U.S. Congress. Congressional committees and subcommittees have jurisdiction over legislation in areas of concentrated benefits, such as agriculture, natural resources, and foreign trade. Committee and subcommittee chairs have much more power than other legislators over legislation under their jurisdiction. The committee system tends to choose chairs whose constituents benefit from legislation under the committee or subcommittee's jurisdiction. For example, agricultural committees and subcommittees normally have chairs who represent heavily agricultural constituencies. The result is excessive government activity in areas where the committee system concentrates legislative power.

Logrolling and coalition formation certainly occur in legislatures. Putting together a set of related proposals that can command the support of a group that is decisive for its passage is the essence of entrepreneurial politics. It is this talent that distinguishes the most powerful members of legislatures in the United States. Nor can there be any doubt that assembling a package of proposals that can command a majority vote rather than a package whose total benefits exceed its total costs is typical behavior. Because a majority is all that is required for passage, legislators have no incentive to find proposals whose total benefits would exceed total costs and would therefore command large majorities. Verification of these ideas really requires little more than a knowledge of the nature of most legislative actions and a careful reading of newspapers to learn how legislators think and act on their jobs. This analysis makes comprehensible the long-standing hostility of legislators to economists' benefit-cost analysis. Economists want to talk about proposals whose total benefits exceed total costs. The majority voting system makes benefit-cost analysis not only irrelevant to legislators' perceptions of their jobs but also a threat to the large governments that their behavior implies and the political incentive system induces them to strive for. Economists typically ascribe legislators' hostility to benefit-cost analysis to the ignorance or perfidy of legislators, but the explanation lies in applying economists' tools of analysis to the legislative system.

However, the previous analysis leaves unclear exactly why logrolling occurs. Return to the numerical example. The coalition that packaged five proposals and secured 55 percent of the vote for them is by no means the only possible coalition. It is worth $0.75 per capita to the 45 percent minority of nonbeneficiaries to prevent adoption of the package of proposals. If the package is not adopted, they save the $0.75 each they must pay in taxes to finance the package if it is adopted. The 45 percent minority could get together and pay one group of 11 people represented by the coalition a bribe of $0.35 each to leave the coalition. To the 55 people represented by the coalition, the net benefit of the package's passage is only $0.25 per capita as the earlier summary shows. Thus, a $0.35 bribe would make any set of 11 voters better off if they were outside rather than inside the coalition. Furthermore, the $0.35 bribe paid to 11 people would cost only $3.85, or less than $0.09 per capita among the 45 people who can share the cost of the bribe. The 45-person minority would certainly be better off because a $0.09 per capita payment would save them $0.75 per capita in losses from passage of the package of proposals.

The notion of paying bribes need not be taken literally. The basic point is that, if legislators accurately represent the interests of con-stituents, there must exist a majority coalition that can defeat any pro-posal that moves society off the utility frontier. But the reverse is also true. A set of proposals exists that can command a majority vote against any set of proposals that would put the society on the utility frontier. In general, no set of proposals exists, on or off the utility frontier, that can command a majority vote against all alternative sets of proposals.[18] This result is not merely an academic point that is correct because bizarre proposals are admitted as possibilities. Even if one proposal has total net benefits that exceed the net benefits of any other proposal and benefits can be transferred freely among voters, it is not generally true that no other proposal can command a majority vote over it. There is no presumption that majority voting by legislators who perfectly represent constituents' interests will result in socially efficient or equitable legislation. Which packages of proposals are legislated seems to depend on institutional details about the organization and procedure of the legislative body.

The basic conclusion of the last few paragraphs is that a legislative process in which legislators represent constituents' interests cannot be expected to produce outcomes or social choices that have desirable char-acteristics—that is, are socially efficient and/or equitable or are even stable. Whatever outcome is chosen, whether good or bad, is likely to be reversed in response to small changes in the membership or organization of the legislative body, to the ways proposals are packaged, or perhaps merely to changes in initial conditions resulting from previous actions of the legislature. This instability of outcomes of the democratic process has led Usher to conclude that restricting the set of issues that is subject to government decision making is crucial to successful functioning of a democracy.[19]

The voting analysis just summarized suggests that government deci-sion making, unrestrained by strong constitutional or other protections, is likely to produce undesirable and unstable results. That conclusion is an important step in explaining the disparity between government decision making and socially efficient resource allocation that seems apparent in modern democratic governments. But nothing in that analysis explains why governments have grown to such excessive sizes and have become increasingly intrusive during the last century or so. That step requires analysis to show why the disparity between government actions and constituents' interests has grown. I turn now to that issue.[20]

The fundamental argument in the literature on this subject is that legislators' behavior need not be closely related to constituents' welfare. If political participation were free of both time and money costs, citizens could vote directly on each issue before the legislature. But political participation is far from free. Elections are costly, but the largest cost is for voters to inform themselves adequately about issues and to choose desirable sets of proposals. The result is that participatory democracy is limited to small groups. In sovereign countries, laws are typically enacted by legislators chosen at infrequent elections. This implies that an enormous range of issues is potentially relevant at a given election. Because large numbers of voters must elect one legislator, it is not possible to match voter interests and legislator platforms closely. Perhaps more important, voters lack the incentive and means to become well informed on more than a few issues. Because elections hardly ever turn on one vote, or on a number of votes that a typical voter might influence, a voter has almost no chance of influencing an election. Voters therefore lack incentive to become informed about issues in elections. And as has been shown, governments lack incentive to inform them.

The result is that elections are fought on the basis of personalities and very general stands that candidates take on a few broad issues. In U.S. congressional elections, issues are of little importance. Hardly any incumbent representatives who are unindicted and choose to stand for reelection fail to be reelected.

A dramatic example of the unimportance of substantive issues in elections in recent U.S. history is afforded by environmental issues. Environmental protection has been intensely political since the 1960s, with enormous amounts of lobbying on all sides, both in Congress and in the national administration. The Environmental Protection Agency was established in 1970 and is now the national government's largest regulatory agency. Yet environmental issues have never been election issues. No serious presidential candidate has made it a significant issue, and it has figured in congressional elections mainly in platitudinous fashion, such as a candidate's promise to "protect the environment without driving jobs out of the jurisdiction." Such platform provisions are merely examples of candidates' efforts to induce the public to underestimate costs of government interventions.

Given that elections impose only mild requirements on legislators to further the interests of constituents, it follows that legislators are free to pursue other goals, within broad limits. One such goal is enlargement of government. Legislators benefit in many ways from large and complex governments. Large and complex government justifies high salaries and large staffs for legislators. Similarly, opportunities are provided for discretionary intervention by legislators to obtain rewards (such as speaking fees and campaign contributions) by furthering goals of interest groups. Jobs are provided both in government and in affected private firms for legislators when they decide to abandon electoral politics.

But the key to the effects of legislative discretion is its effect on interest groups. An ideal interest group consists of people who are easy to organize and who stand to benefit a great deal by potential government actions whose costs can be spread among a large segment of the population, preferably in ways that are difficult to measure. Such groups can "buy" favorable legislation by lobbying, making campaign contributions, provision of favors, offering speaking fees and jobs to legislators, and outright bribery.

Interest groups may be easy to organize because they are small, are geographically concentrated, or have professional identities and perhaps organization or because they have some other form of contact. Members of an interest group stand to benefit most from government actions whose benefits are narrowly focused on group members. Government spending programs are mostly paid for from general government revenues and by deficit financing at the national level. A government spending program worth $100,000 each to half a million members of an interest group can justify a large amount of Washington lobbying. Yet the cost to the average citizen is only about $200. A perfect example is embodied in the federal Davis-Bacon Act and in many similar state laws. Davis-Bacon imposes the apparently innocent requirement that contracts on federal construction projects pay prevailing wages. The contribution of the construction unions was first to induce Congress to pass the law and second to induce the Labor Department to interpret *prevailing* to mean "union." The effect was to foreclose entry in federal building contracts to nonunion contractors. In this example, beneficiaries are identifiable and organized and are able to undertake persistent lobbying in Washington, D.C., and in state capitals. Costs are borne by taxpayers in the form of higher taxes than necessary to pay for construction projects. Costs per taxpayer are small and impossible to calculate.

Much more advantageous are government actions whose costs do not show up on the government budget A government program to license members of an occupation or to limit imports can be very beneficial to members of certain interest groups, yet the costs are reduced efficiency of the economy, which are impossible for those who bear the costs to calculate. Most regulatory programs have the enormous advantage to sponsoring interest groups that they induce voters to underestimate costs of government interventions.

There is hardly any limit to the number of actions governments can take that have large benefits concentrated in small interest groups and much larger total costs dispersed among a large population. The basic requirement is a set of such proposals that can muster a majority in the legislature. The basic constraint on such government actions is that constituents can perceive sufficiently great harm to their own interests, and when they do, they can then elect different legislators. Practical constraints also result from the ability of interest groups to organize and raise money, their ability to reward and punish legislators, the power of particular legislators to influence particular kinds of legislation, and personal and institutional constraints on coalition formation. No one knows how much excessive government results from this defect in the political incentive system. Any conclusion must entail a large element of judgment. Nevertheless, hundreds of federal, state, and local government spending and regulatory programs exist that have large benefits to identifiable groups, although they could hardly make the economy more efficient or equitable.

The most elaborate analysis of the harmful effects of interest group actions is that of Olson, who believes that the gradual accretion of interest groups, each increasing the rigidity and reducing the adaptability of a society and its economy to change, is the major explanation of the decline and fall of societies.[21] Olson explicitly claims that the harmful effects of interest groups can come about without government help to them.[22] He is certainly wrong in this respect. In the absence of government intervention, private groups have incentives to undercut the effects of organized interest groups about in proportion to the harm that interest groups do. For example, the more successful a group of oligopolistic producers is in colluding to raise prices, the greater the incentive that firms (both those that are and those that are not parties to the agreement) have to undercut the collusive agreement. Only the coercive power of government can prevent such undercutting and, therefore, destruction of the agreement and its harmful effects in the long run. Otherwise, Olson's analysis is frighteningly instructive.

The foregoing analysis makes transparent many pervasive characteristics of governments that are otherwise opaque. An important way to reduce the need for governments to further constituents' interests is to conceal actions from them. This accounts for the penchant for secrecy and censorship of governments the world over. Similarly, deficit financing permits governments to spend without the need to levy painful taxes. Deficit-financed spending absorbs resources just as much as spending financed by taxes, but the costs are levied indirectly by inflation, high interest rates, and the like. As a third example, indirect taxes are more difficult for taxpayers to calculate than direct taxes. Individuals can calculate how much income tax they pay, but it is difficult to know how much import duties add to prices of imported products. Finally, governments prefer regulations to direct subsidies for the same reason; costs of regulation are almost impossible to calculate. Governments prefer import controls to direct subsidies paid to domestic producers and regulation of dischargers of polluting wastes to effluent fees. Their only advantage is that the chosen programs obscure costs of government intervention from voters. They prefer crop storage and production control programs to direct subsidies to farmers. They resist use of user fees to finance government production. In all these examples, programs that governments choose are demonstrably worse than easily available alternatives. That taxpayers underestimate not merely the total costs to the economy of government actions but even the taxes they pay is borne out by many studies.[23]

Thousands of interest groups have organized and maintain lobbying offices in Washington, D.C., and in state capitals. In the United States, one of the most important interest groups is government employees, and their influence has been subjected to special analysis. Important references are Niskanen, Tullock, and several papers in Borcherding.[24] The interest of government employees in large and growing government is so obvious as not to require comment. Two distinct aspects of government employees' influence have been studied in the literature.

First, government officials are voters. As governments have grown, government employees have become a significant fraction of the electorate in many jurisdictions. Washington, D.C., is the prime example, but in many large cities, federal, state, and local government employees have significant effects on elections. If one includes recipients of major transfers and voting-age family members of the two groups, this interest group of direct beneficiaries of large government may be nearly a majority of the electorate in some cities. The desire to gather beneficiaries of local government spending in the jurisdiction for voting purposes presumably accounts for laws enacted by many local governments mandating that their employees live in the jurisdiction. The effect is a large block of voters almost guaranteed to vote for large government.

Second, government employees are lobbyists for large governments. Many government employees are unionized. Unions bargain for wages and salaries, employment, and benefits. In addition, they lobby for similar advantages. Associations similar to unions represent most federal government employees and are powerful political forces. Government employees testify and lobby before legislatures for particular programs to enlarge government. Large parts of federal and state governments are taxpayer-financed lobbyists whose function is to further joint interests of government employees and private interest groups. Large parts of the departments of Agriculture, Commerce, Interior, and Labor are in this category in the federal government. More formally, Niskanen has conceived of government agencies as monopoly suppliers of services that must be bought by legislatures.[25] Although government services suppliers do not literally receive profits, they can obtain monopoly benefits in the form of larger organizations and higher salaries than otherwise. But government agencies provide only services they are mandated to provide by legislatures. Perhaps a more realistic view is that legislatures and administrative agencies have joint interests in large governments. The most realistic view is that there is an "iron triangle" of interests among legislators, administrative agencies, and private interest groups in large and intrusive governments.

IMPLICATIONS

Governments and innumerable organized private interest groups have powerful incentives to employ their combined efforts to generate excessively large and intrusive governments, and the democratic process provides only inadequate constraints on government excesses.

The theoretical analysis is persuasive in its logic. But the idea that government serves the interests of specific groups inside and outside government makes transparent an enormous range of otherwise impenetrable facts. It was argued in Chapters 3 through 7 that most spending and regulatory actions of governments are incomprehensible on the usual welfare economics assumption that governments' goals are to further social efficiency and equity. Yet the ways in which spending and regulatory programs further interests of groups inside and outside the government are relatively easy to understand.

Here I return to the broad picture painted earlier in this chapter. The basic point to be made is that my earlier analysis provides powerful reasons to believe that democratic processes produce excessively large governments, but it provides little understanding as to why the constraints on government that were developed slowly and painfully during preceding centuries have gradually failed during the twentieth century. I offer the following interpretation, more as a research agenda than as explanation.

During the last century, the following dramatic changes have been common in presently industrialized and democratic countries: pervasive technical improvements in production of commodities and services, rapidly rising average real incomes, urbanization, and spread of suffrage to virtually all adult citizens.

Rising real incomes have produced much larger surpluses to be extracted by governments for the benefit of politically favored groups. Until the nineteenth century, agricultural land rents constituted most of the surplus that governments could extract. By the late twentieth century, large incomes were generated by an enormous range of production activities; all of these activities generated surpluses to tempt governments and the variety of interest groups they have come to represent.

In the early years of industrialization, even the most democratic countries were controlled by elites who benefited greatly from small governments that intervened only moderately to further the interests of large businesses and a few other dominant groups. As the franchise has spread, many more groups have acquired the ability to influence governments. Such groups are predominantly lower-income than the elites that dominated governments in earlier times, and they stand to gain by an enormous range of government interventions into the private economy.

The ability of governments to control private activity and to extract surpluses has grown. As a result of industrialization and urbanization, land rents have shrunk as a share of GNP. However, economies have become almost completely monetized, which enables governments to require record keeping and reporting of transactions, income, and assets. Government control has also been facilitated by technical improvements in data generation, storage, and retrieval. Such technological improvements, in the form of inexpensive printing, typewriters, carbon paper, mimeograph machines, telephones and telegraph, and office calculators, were important in the nineteenth and early twentieth centuries. Technological change in data handling has, of course, exploded since 1950. Such technical changes facilitate government controls over businesses and households and also enable governments to require private record keeping necessary for large regulatory and tax programs.

Urbanization, resulting from growth of industrial and service sectors, has also been important. Because citizens are spatially concentrated it facilitates control by governments. It also facilitates organization, voting, and lobbying by interest groups intent on extracting favors from

governments. The technological improvements in information generation, storage, and retrieval that were mentioned earlier have also facilitated interest group organization and influence.

Finally, there has been an enormous ideological shift regarding the
proper roles of governments in democratic countries. Until near the end
of the nineteenth century, governments were expected to relate to other
governments, to be domestic referees, and to intervene so as to further
business interests. In the United States, even until the 1930s, courts
frequently prevented government intervention in domestic affairs on
constitutional grounds. Now public ideology is that government should
solve all problems, from unemployment, poverty, and bad harvests to
caring for children, the aged, and the sick and protecting almost every
well-organized group in society from adversity. Courts have become
major instruments of government intervention, on sometimes flimsy
constitutional grounds.[26] Whether this ideological shift is cause, effect, or
both is difficult to know. A history of success by interest groups at
obtaining beneficial government intervention may well breed an ideology favorable to intervention. Likewise, judges' rulings certainly reflect
popular ideological trends, although possibly with long lags.

It seems probable that growth of democratic governments during the
twentieth century is best understood as a result of enlargement of suffrage, growth of incomes and surpluses, and technological change in
production of commodities and services and in information production
and storage and, perhaps most important, as a massive innovation in
political technology and organization.

IMPLICATIONS FOR POOR COUNTRIES

This chapter has been written in the context of a high-
income country, indeed mostly the United States. This concluding section draws implications from the positive theory of government for
low-income countries.

As in rich countries, the key to understanding government behavior
in poor countries is the assumption that government officials, like private
people, try to further their own interests, or improve their own welfare
insofar as constraints imposed on them by the political system permit.
Given that key, the crucial fact is that governments are less democratic in
poor countries than in rich countries, such as the United States. Thus the
constraints on government extraction of surpluses from economic activity are less severe in poor than in rich countries. Likewise, the set of

people whose approval governments need is smaller in nondemocratic and poor countries than in democratic and rich ones.

Measuring the surplus extracted by governments in poor countries is not easy. Government spending of 20 or 25 percent of GNP is a much larger share of total surplus in a poor than in a rich country. But government general spending, discussed in Chapter 8, understates the extraction of surplus from the economy. In many poor countries, for example, governments assume control of large amounts of land (the largest asset in poor countries) in the process of urbanization.[27] This represents surplus extraction by mechanisms other than taxation.

Most contemporary poor countries are highly stratified, with senior government officials and a small set of government supporters typically enjoying much higher living standards than most people. Indeed, all the common measures of income inequality show that poor countries typically have much greater inequality than rich ones.[28]

The positive theory of government and the lack of democratic constraints make distressingly clear why governments in poor countries tax and spend as much as they can and why they resist democratic influences. Democracy is a threat to their control over the economy. It was claimed in Chapter 8 that governments in poor countries also vastly overregulate their economies and, in the process, slow economic growth. It is not quite so obvious what motivates overregulation. After all, there is much more surplus to extract in a prosperous than in a poor economy. Clearly, the power and prestige of political leaders increase with the economy's prosperity. Then why do governments in poor countries impose such a range of formal and informal controls on the private sector even though they impair economic growth and social efficiency?

No theorem says the answer is the same in all countries. Some governments may be too uninformed to understand the consequences of their actions for economic stagnation. In the United States, there seems to be little understanding of the stagnating effect of overregulation, and there is probably less understanding in poor countries. Some governments may be prisoners of antibusiness ideology. But such a pervasive phenomenon cries out for a pervasive explanation.

The only explanation that seems to be consistent with the important facts is that many governments are terrified of economic freedoms. Economic freedoms result in centers of wealth and power that are outside the control of the government. They may provide the resources for private people to help install a different government that is more sympathetic to their needs and interests. In any case, economic freedoms are likely to be followed by demands for political freedoms. The result would be a dramatic loss of power by the government. A wide range of regulatory controls keeps everything under the government's thumb. Such controls prevent emergence of power centers outside the control of the government. They also prevent organization of dissidents and thus prevent dissidents from acquiring enough resources to become a threat to the government.

In fact, several patterns have emerged since World War II. Some African and Latin American governments have tried to maintain tight economic and political control. Some governments—Chile during the 1970s after overthrow of Allende and Taiwan and South Korea with much greater success—have tried to maintain political control while permitting considerable economic freedom. Some governments—such as Brazil, Argentina, and Peru—have combined halting movements toward political freedoms with at least intermittent and partial economic freedom. Perhaps the correct generalization is that governments vary as to their concern with promoting economic growth, and it is not closely correlated with democratic institutions; or perhaps they vary as to how much economic freedom and growth they believe they can permit without loss of political control.

The desire to maintain or achieve political control appears to be the key to understanding the broad outlines of government regulation of economic activity in low-income countries; most regulation appears to have little to do with promotion of social efficiency, economic growth, and equity.

TEN

Conclusions

This book has surveyed and analyzed domestic roles of governments. It has drawn on economic analysis, an array of factual materials, and a large set of studies by other scholars to shed light on the questions: What should governments do? What do they do? and Why do they do what they do?

At every step of the argument, the conclusion has been that governments do much more than is in the interests of their citizens. They spend and regulate far too much. It is true of federal, state, and local governments in the United States, it is true of governments in other industrialized and democratic countries, and it is true of governments in poor countries.

Government excesses impair social efficiency of the economy, slow economic growth, and make the economy less equitable than it should be. In the process, governments deprive citizens of precious economic and political freedoms.

It is widely believed that those who oppose big government are sympathetic to large businesses and lack compassion for the poor. No such logical connection exists. Democratic governments promote the interests of large, well-organized, and well-financed groups. Large businesses qualify on all scores. They had induced governments to further their interests at the sacrifice of average living standards more than a century ago, before almost any other interests had organized and learned to play the political game. To this day, large corporations are among the successful groups in obtaining government favors. But now they have been joined by many other interest groups. Elimination of unjustified government spending and regulatory programs would eliminate programs that benefit large businesses and wealthy unions perhaps more than any other group. The goal of such reforms should be to increase the competitiveness and flexibility of the economy. In the process, entrenched and protected positions of businesses and other institutions would be exposed to competition. Temporarily strong market positions, lasting a few years, can exist as rewards for socially valuable innovations. But strong market positions are self-liquidating, in that the stronger the market position, the greater the incentive for competitors to bid it away. Only with the help of governments can market power be preserved more than the few years it takes for competition to bid it away.

Likewise, regulatory programs are largely for the benefit of well-organized and well-financed industries, occupational groups, and workers. An important effect of many industrial and occupational regulatory programs is to keep out low-income and minority businesses and workers. Elimination of regulatory programs would improve economic opportunities of low income and minority businesses and workers.

Finally, the point of Chapter 4 was that our federal transfer programs are badly organized to serve the needs of the poor. The reform outlined there would focus transfers on the poor to the extent that poverty would be eliminated.

HOW MUCH SHOULD GOVERNMENT SPENDING BE CUT?

Nobody knows how much U.S. government spending could be cut and nevertheless improve economic efficiency and equity. It would take years of research and major elements of judgment to arrive at an answer. Yet it is easy to defend the claim that, in the United States, government domestic spending could be cut at least 50 percent, as a share of GNP, with gains in social efficiency and equity.

To those who follow newspaper accounts of political battles over a few millions of dollars of increased or decreased government spending, the notion of a 50 percent cut in total domestic spending sounds revolutionary. Indeed, it would be revolutionary in political terms. The claim here is that at least half of domestic government spending in the United States must be understood in political terms and has nothing to do with economic efficiency or equity.

In 1983, total government spending in the United States was 35.4

percent of GNP. Military and international spending was 6.6 percent of GNP, leaving 28.8 percent of GNP for the remainder. Net interest payments of all governments were 2.2 percent of GNP. Interest payments result from borrowing, and it is meaningless to say that they result from domestic or international spending. Nevertheless, reductions in domestic spending and more sensible macroeconomic policies would, as discussed in Chapter 5, result in smaller deficits and lower real interest rates. Both would reduce interest payments as a share of GNP within a few years. Thus interest payments are certainly among the items that would be cut if domestic government spending were cut. However, it is impossible to say by how much government interest payments would fall as a share of GNP. Even ignoring effects on government interest payments, a 50 percent cut in domestic government spending would lower government spending from something like 27 to something like 13.5 percent of GNP.[1]

To place the discussion in perspective, total government domestic spending was 13.9 percent of GNP in 1949. Indeed, government interest payments were about 1.7 percent of GNP. Thus a 50 percent cut in domestic spending by government in 1983 would leave government domestic spending at about the share of GNP that it was as recently as 1949, whether one includes or excludes interest payments in the comparison.[2] There is no reason to believe that government spending cuts should be precisely those that have been added since 1949. The comparison of government spending after a suggested cut of 50 percent with government spending in 1949 is merely meant to suggest that the proposed cuts would nevertheless leave large governments and large government domestic spending in the United States.

It has already been shown, in Chapter 4, that reform of government transfer programs could reduce them by about 50 percent, from about 11 to about 5 percent of GNP, while improving equity and, perhaps, social efficiency. At the federal government level, reductions on the order of 50 percent could be made in transportation, agricultural, health, housing, energy, and education programs. The largest expenditures in agricultural programs are disguised transfers that reduce social efficiency and lack an equity justification. Most energy expenditures are unjustified regulatory or subsidy programs. Virtually all housing programs should be abolished. Some have had no social benefits, and none has a benefit-cost ratio as large as 1. Transportation programs that cannot be financed with user fees should be abolished. Most federal health subsidies should be ended. Similar percentage but smaller absolute reductions could be made in programs of the departments of Commerce, Interior, and Labor. The departments of Energy and Education should be abolished. Remaining programs in Energy could be transferred to a department created by combining remaining programs in Commerce and Labor. Virtually all federal regulatory agencies should be abolished. Introduction of simple economic incentives would permit the largest, the Environmental Protection Agency, to be drastically cut.

At the state and local levels, spending could be reduced by elimination of nearly all regulatory programs. Likewise, reprivatization of the health care system would reduce federal, state, and local government spending and would permit improvements in social efficiency. Smaller reductions could be made in many other state and local government programs. A major issue in state and local government spending is education, which accounts for 25 percent of all state and local government spending. There is no reason for state and local governments to operate a large and expensive system of higher education institutions. They achieve almost no income redistribution from the nonpoor to the poor. They could be converted to private institutions with the advantage of large reductions in state and local government spending. States could, if they wished, provide financial assistance to qualified low-income students at a fraction of what they now spend on higher education.

From the point of view of welfare economics, it is difficult to doubt that elementary and secondary education should be based on a voucher system. All parents would receive, for each of their children, vouchers that could be used for either public or private schools. Although the immediate impact on government educational spending would be small, the advantage of competition among educational institutions would be great. Considerable savings would result in the long run, as competition forced down salaries and administrative staff; but it is impossible to know how much the savings would be. Finally, the United States simply has too many local governments. Large numbers should be abolished.

It would be naive to think that a reduction in government domestic spending anywhere near the 50 percent target suggested here could be made within a few years. It took a century to achieve the present excessive sizes of governments. The time required to reduce governments to desirable sizes must be measured in decades. It was shown in Chapter 4 that replacement of social security and other federal transfer programs by a more equitable transfer program would require a two- or three-decade transition. In addition, rapid reduction would be disruptive to the private sector.

Reduction of government domestic spending from 27 to 13.5 percent of GNP would not entail directly a 13.5 percent increase in living standards. That would happen only if there were no private benefit from present high levels of government spending. For example, most reductions in transfer payments would need to be replaced in part by increases in private spending mostly financed by resources freed by resulting reductions in taxes and deficit spending. As another example, part of the reduced spending of state and local governments on higher education would need to be replaced by private spending. Again, reduced government spending would free resources that could be employed by private spending. Benefits would be generated by greater competition, greater freedom of choice among educational institutions, and by removal of distortions, such as excessive enrollments, induced by underpricing higher education.

The benefits of reductions in sizes of governments would come from greater competition, greater freedom of choice, reduced distortions from excessive regulation and excessive taxes, better matching of production to consumer tastes and needs, lower-cost production, and improved incentives to innovate. Those benefits would be real and substantial; they would be much greater in the long than in the short run. Beyond doubt, reduced regulation and distortions from government spending and taxing would raise the national growth rate. A doubling of the growth rate of real per capita GNP, back to its level in the 1950s and early 1960s, would be a realistic expectation and would soon result in much higher average living standards. But it would be naive to put precise dollar values on short-run or long-run benefits of reduced government spending.

REDUCING GOVERNMENT REGULATION

Measured by amounts government spend, much more than half of all government regulation should be abolished. But government administrative costs are only a small part of the savings that would result from abolishing regulatory programs. Not only the small army of government regulatory officials but also the similar and corresponding small army of people employed by the private sector to comply with regulations could be freed for socially useful work. In addition, distortions because of regulation would be removed.

My judgment is that the greatest benefit of reductions in regulation would be the increased competitiveness, flexibility, and innovativeness of the private sector. It seems likely than an important part of the deceleration of economic growth during the 1970s in the United States and elsewhere resulted from excessive government regulation. Finally, public confidence in the private sector is undermined by its poor performance resulting from overregulation. Regulation almost inevitably breeds more regulation.

IMPROVING EQUITY

It is extremely difficult to convince people that government spending and regulation can be drastically curtailed at the same time that government improves equity. Compassionate people justify the most wasteful government programs on the grounds that, somehow, they provide at least a little help to low-income people. In fact, the U.S. political system is one in which any powerful and well-organized group can extract transfers or protection of economic positions from governments. In such a system, government spending and regulation do not substantially protect the poor.

From 1960 to 1982, real transfer expenditures of governments to people increased more than 7 percent per year and were 4.5 times as great in 1982 as in 1960. During that time, the percentage of the population that was below the poverty line, by the government's measure, fell only from 22 to 15. That represents a slower shrinkage rate of the percentage in poverty than the average growth rate of real income per capita.[3] Neither U.S. government transfer programs nor any other programs have been targeted effectively on the poor. Wasteful programs mainly produce waste, not equity.

As a matter of welfare economics, a government transfer program that completely eliminated involuntary poverty in the United States would be easy to formulate and finance. As was shown in Chapter 4, a tolerably well-targeted transfer program with good incentives for self-help could eliminate poverty completely with a total government expenditure of no more than 5 percent of GNP, about half the current GNP share of transfers.

IMPLEMENTATION

If it is possible to cut government spending by 50 percent, eliminate most government regulation, and improve government equity programs—and if the effects would be to accelerate economic growth and improve the social efficiency and flexibility of the economy—why do we and other industrialized countries not do it?

The positive theory of government, discussed in Chapter 9, implies that the answer is that, in most democracies, the political incentives are inappropriate. They enable elected and appointed government officials to combine with well-organized private groups to establish government spending, regulatory and transfer programs that benefit government officials and particular private groups, but do so at the expense of average living standards and impaired competition and incentives. With large numbers of private groups extracting benefits from government, the effect is that average living standards are much lower than they would be if government followed more enlightened policies, growth is stifled, the economy loses its flexibility and competitiveness, economic and political freedoms are lost, and equity is hardly better and possibly worse.

Having gotten this far, many people throw up their hands in pessimism, concluding that excessively large governments are the inevitable result of democracy with a broad franchise. I am not so pessimistic.

One need is for a more enlightened electorate. Although most people appear to believe that governments are excessively large and intrusive, many people are unconvinced that great harm has resulted. Education is the only answer a scholar can propose to improve public enlightenment.

Better public understanding of the harm done by excessively large governments cannot be the entire recipe for a solution. Suppose everyone knew that a particular set of government actions would benefit government and particular private groups, but at the expense of average living standards. It was shown in Chapter 9 that governments and individual groups are motivated in their self-interest to combine and advocate such programs despite their overall negative net benefits. Furthermore, under rules and traditions of government decision making that are common in democracies, such combinations of government and private groups can be decisive in inducing governments to adopt programs that have positive net benefits to the group, although their net benefits to the entire population are negative.

Then, even though each government–private interest group coalition knows the social harm its favorite program will do, each such coalition is motivated to induce government to adopt the program. It was claimed in Chapter 9 that adoption of programs that enlarge governments satisfies strong predilections of important government officials. Furthermore, in the context of late twentieth-century democracies, each private interest group can rationally justify socially costly enlargement of government for its benefit. Many other groups are feeding at the public trough and will continue to do so whether any particular group feeds or not. Thus, if one group does not feed, it will be left out; but enough other groups will feed so that about as much social damage will be done anyway. That is a rational and irresistible argument to almost any group.

The foregoing makes clear that even complete understanding of the harm done by excessive government would not induce people to change their political behavior. What is needed is a different set of rules by which democracies transform citizens' interests and wishes into government actions. Appropriate rules would need to restrain combinations of private interest groups and government organizations from enlarging government at the expense of average living standards.

I do not know what set of decision-making rules (or *constitution*, to use the academically fashionable term), would be optimum. Nor do I know what set of political actions, if any, can result in optimum rules. The latter problem is especially difficult, given the argument in the preceding chapter that, unless constrained by the political process, government officials generate excessive government spending and regulation.

However, the following argument provides cause for some optimism. If the contentions of this book are correct, the rules for government decision making have placed the economy well inside the long-run utility frontier. If so, there exists a different set of rules for government decision making that can make everybody better off. Thus the move from the existing to the optimum set of rules should command unanimous approval.

The foregoing is an abstract and naive statement. No major change in human institutions can literally make everyone better off or command unanimous approval of a large and diverse group of people. Furthermore, various groups in a political system can prevent particular changes, given the rules under which system operates. The statement is merely meant to suggest that it is not naive to think that present rules can be changed for the better.

Notes

CHAPTER 1

1. Richard Just, Darrell Heuth, and Andrew Schmitz, *Applied Welfare Economics and Public Policy* (Englewood Cliffs, N.J.: Prentice-Hall, 1982), is the best.

2. Textbooks tend to say "Situation X provides the person more utility than situation Y" or "X places the person on a higher indifference curve than Y" instead of "X is preferred to Y." Except for unimportant technicalities, the three statements have the same meaning. A utility function is simply a way of attaching numbers to situations such that a situation has a higher utility number if, and only if, it is preferred.

3. Thus social efficiency requires only that no other resource allocation exist that enables one or more people to attain preferred situations without putting one or more others in less preferred situations. No common units for people's utilities or welfare are required.

4. See Chapter 2 of Just, Heuth, and Schmitz, *Welfare Economics and Public Policy*.

CHAPTER 2

1. Government spending on transfer payments as well as on goods and services is included, where available. Government spending in government-owned industries is included only to the extent that it is financed from the government budget and not from sales of goods and services.

2. See William McNeill, *The Pursuit of Power* (Chicago: University of Chicago Press, 1982).

3. Statistics in this paragraph are calculated from U.S. Council of Economic Advisers, *Economic Report to the President* (Washington, D.C.: U.S. Government Printing Office, 1984) and U.S. Census Bureau, *Historical Statistics of the United States* (Washington, D.C.: U.S. Government Printing Office, 1975).

4. Statistics in this paragraph are from Tax Foundation, Inc., *Facts and Figures on Government Finance* (Washington, D.C.: Tax Foundation, 1983, Table 149). Small transfers are made from revenues raised directly by state government to local governments. They are included in the state share in Table 3.

CHAPTER 3

1. Confusion can be avoided by consideration of a third example. Suppose *A* agrees to pay *B* if *B* builds a garage for *A*. *B* builds the garage, but *A* decides not to pay *B*. *B* sues, and the court forces *A* to pay *B*. As used here, the term *coercion* will not be applied to the court's action. For the purposes of this book, no distinction is needed between the making and execution of voluntary agreements, so the notion of coerced enforcement of voluntary agreement is not needed.

2. Such laws entail a form of coercion. It could be said that governments coerce people not to coerce others. An ideal set of laws induces people to behave so that society reaches the utility frontier. Even if that happened, it would be in the interests of some people to violate the laws (for example, by stealing other people's money), even though it moved the society away from the utility frontier by distorting allocations of time and resources. Such coercion not to coerce is not the main subject of this book.

3. Of course, it is possible to move from any point off the utility frontier to points on the utility frontier at which some people are worse off. But starting from any point off the utility frontier, it is, by definition, possible to move to the utility frontier—that is, to achieve social efficiency—without making anyone worse off. Because such moves are possible, it should be possible to achieve social efficiency without coercion.

4. See Lawrence Friedman, *A History of American Law* (New York: Simon & Schuster, 1973).

5. That is, the part left after paying taxes necessary to finance justifiable government activity.

6. Some of the best recent papers on the subjects discussed in this section are in Steven Lin, ed., *Theory and Measurement of Economic Externalities* (Orlando, Fla.: Academic Press, 1976). See also Robert Haveman and Julius Margolis, eds., *Public Expenditure and Policy Analysis.* (Boston: Houghton Mifflin, 1983).

7. See the paper by Arrow in Haveman and Margolis, *Public Expenditure and Policy Analysis.*

8. It may, of course, be worthwhile to acquire more information concerning a large transaction than concerning a small one. The statement in the text refers to the technology of information gathering, not to incentives to acquire much or little information.

9. See Richard Just, Darrell Heuth, and Andrew Schmitz, *Applied Welfare Economics and Public Policy* (Englewood Cliffs, N.J.: Prentice-Hall, 1982), pp. 283–86.

10. As frequently occurs, technology has replaced lighthouses with electronic devices for which exclusion is easy.

11. See M. A. Satterthwaite, "Strategy-Proofness and Arrow's Conditions: Existence and Correspondence Theorems for Voting Procedures and Social Welfare Functions," *Journal of Economic Theory* 10 (1975): 182–213.

12. The statistics in this paragraph are from Nation Science Board, *Science Indicators 1980* (Washington, D.C.: National Science Foundation, 1981).

13. Equivalently, total input productivity increases with output, or the elasticity of output with respect to a proportionate increase in all inputs exceeds 1.

14. Social efficiency in a natural monopoly requires a price-quantity combination determined by the intersection of the demand and marginal-cost curves. The resulting losses should be financed in some way other than by sale of the product. One socially efficient scheme is to finance losses by a lump-sum payment that permits a customer to buy at the marginal-cost price. This is referred to as a two-part tariff.

15. On the benefits of potential competition in markets where some element of natural monopoly is present, see William Baumol, John Panzer, and Robert Willig, *Contestable Markets and the Theory of Industry Structure* (New York: Harcourt Brace Jovanovich, 1982).

16. Just, Heuth, and Schmitz, *Applied Welfare Economics and Public Policy*, is a fine survey of the subject.

17. Potentially, the other most important application is to technical progress resulting from research and development. But little progress has been made in this application.

18. This statement requires assumptions about technology and utility functions that guarantee an interior solution. Typically, such assumptions seem to be satisfied.

19. See Lawrence White, *Reforming Regulation* (Englewood Cliffs, N.J.: Prentice-Hall, 1981). Benefit-cost analysis seems hardly to have entered the purview of state and local governments.

20. Government techniques of benefit-cost analysis cannot be surveyed here. One dramatic example is that some government benefit-cost studies assume, without evidence or analysis, that a large percentage of those who would be

employed on a proposed project would have been unemployed in the absence of the project. For that group, labor costs are valued at zero instead of at wages paid because it is assumed that those workers would have had no earnings in the absence of the project. Thus the social opportunity cost of employing them on the project is assumed to be zero.

21. On this subject, see Henry Aaron, *Politics and the Professors* (Washington, D.C.: Brookings Institution, 1978).

22. That discharges are to be abated by the "best available technology" is a good example.

23. See Benjamin Lippincott, ed., *On the Economic Theory of Socialism* (Minneapolis: University of Minnesota Press, 1948) and Abba Lerner, *The Economics of Control* (New York: Macmillan, 1944).

24. The purpose of this institutional framework is to achieve resource allocation that would be achieved by competitive markets, but under conditions of technology that might not permit competitive markets. It has been shown in the text of this chapter that competitive profit maximization might not get the economy to the utility frontier—because of public-goods problems, for example. That would be equally true of the socialist scheme discussed here. However, motivating managers to comply with any goal set for a production unit by the planning board would be equally difficult if the manager did not benefit from achievement of the goal.

25. Galbraith, J. Kenneth. *The New Industrial State*. Boston: Houghton Mifflin, 1967.

CHAPTER 4

1. Tax specialists debate what tax system has the least possible effect on resource allocation. At the most abstract level, it might depend on lifetime income if the taxpayer engages in socially efficient use of time and property throughout life. Because no one knows just what each person's socially efficient accumulation and use of human and physical capital is, one is driven to use of proxies. A tax proportionate to consumption appears to be the closest practically possible to the ideal. A flat rate income tax—tax payments proportionate to income—might be administratively simpler and is favored by some specialists. Tax systems presently used in the United States and in most countries bear little relationship to tax systems grounded in welfare economics. Existing tax systems are loaded with gimmicks intended to further interests of governments (for example, by concealing the magnitude of taxes) and to further the interests of particular interest groups. Existing tax systems can be understood only in the context of the positive theory of government discussed in Chapter 9.

Although any practically possible tax system affects private resource allocation, if the government raises revenues of an amount, and by a tax system, that permits resource allocation to be socially efficient, or as nearly so as possible, then the tax system should not be thought of as distorting.

2. Competition is the key process in eliminating profits in excess of competitive equilibrium returns to capital. In an economy with free entry into industries, most profits in excess of competitive returns to capital are short-run rewards for unusually valuable innovations. They are eliminated by entry of competitors within a few years. As pointed out in Chapter 3, various cooperative and other voluntary arrangements would generate socially efficient resource allocation in activities in which technology does not permit adequate competition. In cases of increasing returns at optimum output, optimum pricing of outputs and inputs entails losses. In most cases, losses can be made up by two-part tariffs. With pure public goods, membership fees can usually provide a good approximation to economists' ideal of resource allocation. Decreasing returns to scale at optimum output and with optimum output and input prices entails profits in excess of competitive returns to capital. Normally, the high costs at output levels associated with decreasing returns can be avoided by production with large numbers of small production units instead of with small numbers of large production units. If technology permits competition, it provides the optimum number of optimum-sized production units.

3. See World Bank, *World Development Report 1984* (New York: Oxford University Press, 1984).

4. Elasticities of substitution between capital and labor are typically less than 1. This implies that the income share of capital falls as its quantity rises relative to that of labor.

5. See Edwin Mills and Charles Becker, "Urbanization, Public Services, and Income Distribution in Developing Countries," in B. Prantilla, ed., *National Development and Regional Policy* (Singapore: Maruzan Asia for the U.N. Center for Regional Development, 1981), pp. 57–70, on the subject of this paragraph.

6. For an account of the effects of transfers on the recipients, see Charles Murray, *Losing Ground* (New York: Basic Books, 1984).

7. Among those who appear willing to tolerate relatively great inefficiency are Arthur Okun, *Equality and Efficiency: The Big Tradeoff* (Washington, D.C.: Brookings Institution, 1975) and John Rawls, *A Theory of Justice* (Cambridge, Mass.: Belknap Press of the Harvard University Press, 1971).

8. For example, Ray Fair, "The Optimal Distribution of Income," *Quarterly Journal of Economics* 85, no. 4 (November 1971): 551–79, and James Mirrlees, "Arguments for Public Expenditure," in M. J. Artis and A. R. Nobay, eds., *Contemporary Economic Analysis* (London: Croom Helm, 1978), pp. 273–99.

9. For the definition and analysis of public goods, see Chapter 3. For the notion that income redistribution is a public good, see Lester Thurow, "The Income Redistribution as a Pure Public Good," *Quarterly Journal of Economics* 85, no. 2 (May 1971): 327–36. For criticisms of the concept, see subsequent issues of the *Quarterly Journal*.

10. See Dan Usher, *The Economic Prerequisites of Democracy* (New York: Columbia University Press, 1981).

11. See Joel Slemrod, "Do We Know How Progressive the Income Tax System Should Be?" *National Tax Journal* 36, no. 3 (1983): 361–69.

12. See Sheldon Danziger, Robert Haveman, and Robert Plotnick, "How Income Transfers Affect Work, Savings, and the Income Distribution," *Journal of Economic Literature* 19, no. 3 (September 1981): 975–1028, and Charles Murray, *Losing Ground* (New York: Basic Books, 1984) and references therein.

13. See U.S. Council of Economic Advisers, *Economic Report to the President* (Washington, D.C.: U.S. Government Printing Office, 1984).

14. See Danziger, Haveman, and Plotnick, "Income Transfers," 975–1028, and Murray, *Losing Ground.*

15. Difficulties arise as to treatment of children in any transfer program. Payments for children would be made to legal guardians. My suggestion is that the payment for a child increase from $150 to $250 per month when the child reaches 18 years of age. Payment for a child would cease to depend on the income of the parents' family and would depend on the income of the child or the child's family when the child married, reached age 21, or ceased to be a full-time student, whichever came first.

16. Private income would include earnings, property income, and private transfers, such as alimony and child support. For married couples, private income would include income of all family members.

17. The calculation is based on the assumption that transfers per capita are the same for unrelated individuals as for family members at a given per capita income. Even if the figure is off by 50 percent, it makes little difference to the estimate of total program cost.

18. The income tax figure from the U.S. Internal Revenue Service's *Statistics of Income, Personal Income Tax Returns, 1980* (Washington, D.C.: U.S. Department of Justice, 1983) refers to 1980, the latest year for which tax data are available at the time of writing. The figure is total income tax paid by those whose adjusted gross income was less than $15,000. Tax reductions since then imply that people in these brackets now pay less tax. Under the proposed program, social security taxes and benefits would be abolished. Some social security taxes are paid by those who would be eligible for negative-income tax payments under the plan described in the text, and some are paid by higher-income people. Social security taxes paid in 1980 cannot easily be calculated precisely but are probably of amounts similar to income taxes they pay.

19. Participation in all transfer programs is voluntary, and not all those legally eligible choose to participate in any program. Some people choose not to participate because they find transfers degrading or because their incomes are high enough or their anticipated eligibility is short enough that the amount they would receive does not justify the bother of participating. Of course, reasonable efforts should be made to inform people of program benefits and eligibility criteria. But if people choose not to participate, it is their right. In addition, a few people are

unable to participate because of physical or mental handicaps. Relations and friends can help, but governments simply must be legal guardian for others.

CHAPTER 5

1. For government restrictions on occupational and industrial mobility of labor, see Chapters 6 and 7. It is obvious that there is much short-run disequilibrium among employed people. Most of it results from short-run immobility of workers and firms and from the difficulty in acquiring precise information about job openings and worker availability. No evidence or analysis suggests that government intervention alleviates these problems. For example, few people find jobs through government employment exchanges.

2. In the early 1980s, the federal government used a measured unemployment rate of 6 percent as the full employment target.

3. Monetary economists disagree as to what money supply concept is most relevant to measure government stabilization policy. The measure employed in Table 10 is the least inclusive of those published by the Federal Reserve and has grown least rapidly during the period for which the data have been published.

4. See William Baumol and Kenneth McLennan, eds., *Stimulating U.S. Productivity Growth* (New York: Oxford University Press, 1985), and references therein.

5. See Arthur Okun, *Equality and Efficiency: The Big Tradeoff* (Washington, D.C.: Brookings Institution, 1975), for a fuller account.

CHAPTER 6

1. See Sam Peltzman, "An Evaluation of Consumer Protection Legislation: The 1962 Drug Amendments," *Journal of Political Economy* 81, no. 5, (September–October 1973): 1049–91.

2. This portion of the chapter draws heavily on Murray Weidenbaum, *Business, Government, and the Public* (Englewood Cliffs, N.J.: Prentice-Hall, 1981).

3. Weidenbaum, *Business, Government, and the Public*, p. 26.

4. Any good textbook on industrial organization or government regulation provides many examples. Many papers analyzing postwar regulatory programs appear in *Journal of Law and Economics* and in *Journal of Public Economics*. Such studies also appear in other economics journals.

5. For a study of delays in railroad innovation caused by ICC, see Paul Macavoy and James Sloss, *Regulation of Transport Innovation* (New York: Random House, 1963).

6. See Weidenbaum, *Business, Government, and the Public*, for more information on this subject.

7. The best summary of the skeptical view is George Stigler, *The Citizen and the State* (Chicago: University of Chicago Press, 1975).

8. See Edwin Mills and Philip Graves, *The Economics of Environmental Quality* (New York: Norton, 1986) for a survey and references.

9. See Mills and Graves, *Economics of Environmental Quality*, for a summary of relevant studies. At the abatement level at which total costs and benefits of abatement are equal, costs must be rising faster than benefits, so marginal costs and benefits are equated at a lesser amount of abatement.

10. Weidenbaum, *Business, Government, and the Public*, pp. 342–44.

11. See Lawrence Friedman, *A History of American Law* (New York: Simon & Schuster, 1973).

CHAPTER 7

1. Congressional Quarterly, Inc., *Federal Regulatory Directory, 1983–84.* (Washington, D.C.: Congressional Quarterly, 1983), Council of State Governments, *Book of the States*, vol. 24, 1982–83 (Lexington, Ky.: Council of State Governments, 1982), and Nancy Wright and Gene Allen, *National Directory of State Agencies 1982–83* (Arlington, Va.: Information Resources Press, 1982).

2. General sources of information for this discussion are Council of State Governments, *Book of the States*, and Wright and Allen, *Directory of State Agencies*. The historical growth of state and local government regulation is traced in Lawrence Friedman, *A History of American Law* (New York: Simon & Schuster, 1973).

3. There is a large anecdotal literature on this subject. See Henry Peskin, Paul Portney, and Allen Kneese, eds., *Environmental Regulation and the U.S. Economy* (Baltimore, Md.: Johns Hopkins University Press for Resources for the Future, 1981), and especially, the paper by Harrington and Krupnick and references therein.

4. A good survey for New York City is in Harold Hochman's "The Over-Regulated City: A Perspective on Regulatory Procedures in New York City, *Public Finance Quarterly* 9, no. 2 (April 1981): 197, 219.

5. A large set of empirical studies was spawned by John Crecine, Otto Davis, and John Jackson, "Urban Property Markets: Some Empirical Results and Their Implications for Municipal Zoning," *Journal of Law and Economics* 10 (1967): 29–100.

6. The 1970 correlation between per capita local government taxes and population of the locality was about .31. Readers can convince themselves of the accuracy of the statement in the text by glancing at Table 483 of U.S. Census Bureau, *Statistical Abstract of the United States 1982–83* (Washington, D.C.: U.S. Government Printing Office, 1984).

7. Charles Tiebout, "A Pure Theory of Local Public Expenditures," *Journal of Political Economy* 64 (1956): 416–24.

8. Other assumptions are needed to ensure social efficiency. Jurisdictions must be large enough to exhaust scale economies in production of local government services. Services for which scale economies are too great, such as water supply and sewage disposal, are usually provided by consortia of local governments or by state government agencies. Studies reported and referred to in George Zodrow, ed., *Local Provision of Public Services: The Tiebout World After Twenty-Five Years* (Orlando, Fla.: Academic Press, 1983), indicate that scale economies of services provided by local governments are exhausted even in quite small jurisdictions. In addition, there must not be interjurisdictional spillovers, in which one local government's actions affect the welfare of people in neighboring jurisdictions. That is why local governments are given almost no responsibility for environmental protection. Thus both assumptions are innocuous as to services provided by local governments, but tell us a great deal about why particular services are provided at one level of government or another.

9. See George Zodrow, ed., *Local Provision of Public Services: The Tiebout World After Twenty-Five Years* (Orlando, Fla.: Academic Press, 1983) and references therein.

10. See the paper by Hamilton in Zodrow, *Local Provision of Public Services*.

11. Thomas Hagler, ed., "Land Use and Housing in the San Francisco Peninsula," Stanford Environmental Law Annual 4, (1982). Stanford, Calif.: Stanford Environmental Law Society, 1983.

12. To avoid confusion, licenses for drivers are referred to as *licenses* and those for vehicles are referred to by the local New York name, *medallions*.

13. In Figure 1, price is revenue per taxi, not a measure of fares. If taxis are used about the same number of hours per day, fares translate mechanically into revenue per taxi. If medallion restrictions were removed, taxis might be used fewer hours per day. That would have to be taken into account in calculating the effect of removing the restrictions on the number of taxis.

CHAPTER 8

1. Gunnar Myrdal, *Asian Drama* (New York: Twentieth Century Fund, 1968).

2. Among the saddest intellectual spectacles of our time is the band of international development conference itinerants—scholars, public officials, journalists—who go from one conference to another, many under U.N. sponsorship, urging more comprehensive government economic planning.

3. See Irving Kravis, Alan Heston, and Robert Summers, *World Production and Income* (Baltimore, Md.: Johns Hopkins University Press, 1982). These data

adjust GNP per capita in various ways to provide better comparisons of living standards.

4. World Bank, *World Development Report 1984* (New York: Oxford University Press, 1984).

5. See Charles L. Taylor, ed., *Why Governments Grow* (Beverly Hills, Calif.: Sage, 1983), for one of the best.

6. See Sam Peltzman, "The Growth of Government," *Journal of Law and Economics* 23, no. 2 (October 1980): 209–88, and references therein.

7. World Bank, *World Development Report, 1984* (New York: Oxford University Press, 1984).

8. See Harold Dunkerley, ed., *Urban Land Policy* (New York: Oxford University Press, 1983).

9. Careful studies conclude that social returns to education exceed those to investment in physical capital in poor countries. See Timothy King, ed., *Education and Income* (Washington, D.C.: World Bank Staff Working Paper No. 402, 1980), and references therein.

10. Development of sophisticated financial institutions at early stages of development in such places as Singapore and Hong Kong shows that private institutions develop if governments permit them to. During the 1970s, the National Bureau of Economic Research published twelve volumes on foreign trade regimes in developing countries. Most contain descriptions of government financial controls in the countries studied.

11. In some countries, multinational firms can bring funds from abroad. See the discussion of import controls later in this chapter.

12. See, for example, Jagdish Baghwati and Padma Desai, *India: Planning for Industrialization* (London: Oxford University Press, 1970).

13. See Uday Sekhar, *Industrial Location Policy: The Indian Experience* (Washington, D.C.: World Bank Staff Working Paper No. 620, 1983).

14. On the harm done by excessive wages (mostly government controlled) in developing countries, see Michael Todaro, *Economic Development in the Third World* (New York: Longman, 1981).

15. See Johannes Linn, *Cities in the Developing World* (New York: Oxford University Press for the World Bank, 1983).

16. See Anne Krueger, *Foreign Trade Regimes and Economic Development: Liberalization Attempts and Consequences* (Cambridge, Mass.: Ballinger, 1978).

17. See Malcolm Gillis, Dwight Perkins, Michael Roemer, and Donald Snodgrass, *Economics of Development* (New York: Norton, 1983).

18. The legal device is loans to governments from their central banks. Deficits are also financed on a large scale by foreign borrowing.

19. See William McNeill, *The Pursuit of Power* (Chicago: University of Chicago Press, 1982), for a broad historical account.

20. Free trade would prevent government from setting exchange rates arbitrarily, which would also be desirable.

CHAPTER 9

1. Anthony Downs, *An Economic Theory of Democracy* (New York: Harper, 1957).

2. James Buchanan and Gordon Tullock, *The Calculus of Consent* (Ann Arbor: University of Michigan Press, 1962).

3. For examples, see Thomas Borcherding, ed., *Budgets and Governments: Sources of Government Growth* (Durham, N.C.: Duke University Press, 1977); G. Warren Nutter, *Growth of Government in the West* (Washington, D.C.: American Enterprise Institute, 1978); and Sam Peltzman, "The Growth of Government," *Journal of Law and Economics* 23, no. 2 (October 1980): 209–88.

4. See E. Jones, *The European Miracle* (Cambridge, Eng.: Cambridge University Press, 1981).

5. This seems now to be a common view among historians. It has been developed and documented by, among others, William McNeill in his *Pursuit of Power* (Chicago: University of Chicago Press, 1982).

6. The production function characteristics that generate nearly constant shares are nearly constant returns to scale and nearly unit elasticities of substitution between pairs of inputs.

7. See P. Yotopoulos and J. Nugent, *Economics of Development: Empirical Investigations* (New York: Harper and Row, 1976), for production function estimates. Many studies have documented agricultural shares accruing to landlords. See I. J. Singh, *Small Farmers and the Landless in South Asia* (Washington, D.C.: World Bank, 1982. Mimeographed), and references therein.

8. Although the landlord's share of agricultural output may hardly be affected by workers' wages, the larger the labor force and the lower the wage rate per worker, the larger the total rent per acre.

9. See Jones, *The European Miracle*. Many historical studies contain fragmentary evidence that suggests a similar distribution between agricultural workers and recipients of rents and taxes.

10. See Jones, *The European Miracle*, for a provocative account of this process.

11. Lest the contagion effect of democracy and government restraint be overestimated, it should be emphasized that it has still not spread to the vast majority of countries of the world.

12. It also suggests the hypothesis that nondemocratic governments undertake armed conquest, which has dominated history, whenever additional surplus to which it would provide access exceeds the cost of the conquest. Presumably, democratic governments are constrained to place a higher value on lives than nondemocrataic governments.

13. William Baumol, "Macroeconomics of Unbalanced Growth: The Anatomy of the Urban Crisis," *American Economic Review* 57 (June 1967): 415–26.

14. See Thomas Borcherding, "The Sources of Growth Public Expenditures" (in Borcherding, *Budgets and Governments*).

15. Several papers in William Baumol and Kenneth McLennan, eds., *Stimulating U.S. Productivity Growth* (New York: Oxford University Press, 1985), analyze reasons for the slow growth of productivity in government service provision.

16. Buchanan and Tullock, *Calculus of Consent*; Milton Friedman and Rose Friedman, *Free to Choose* (New York: Harcourt Brace Jovanovich, 1980); George Stigler, *The Citizen and the State* (Chicago: University of Chicago Press, 1975); Peltzman, "Growth of Government," pp. 209–88); and Harold Demsetz, "Why Regulate Utilities?" *Journal of Law and Economics* 11, (April 1968): 55–65.

17. Buchanan and Tullock, *Calculus of Consent*; Gordon Tullock, *Private Wants, Public Means* (New York: Basic Books, 1970); and Gordon Tullock, *The Social Dilemma* (Blacksburg, Va.: Center for Study of Public Choice, 1974).

18. The technical statement is that the core is empty for majority voting games. In fact, all politically interesting majority voting games seem to have empty cores. See Gerald Kramer, "Theories of Political Processes," in Michael Intrilligator, ed., *Frontiers of Quantitative Economics*, Vol. 3 (Amsterdam: North-Holland, 1974), and Dennis Mueller, *Public Choice* (Cambridge, Eng.: Cambridge University Press, 1979).

19. See Dan Usher, *The Economic Prerequisites of Democracy* (New York: Columbia University Press, 1981). The basic mathematical analysis is known as the Gibbard-Satterthwaite analysis. See M. A. Satterthwaite, "Strategy-Proofness and Arrow's Conditions: Existence and Correspondence Theorems for Voting Procedures and Social Welfare Functions," *Journal of Economic Theory* 10 (1975): 182–83, and references therein. The basic mathematical model is so general that it applies to any method of resource allocation achieved by a given set of participants in the decision-making process. Some economists believe that the analysis undermines the conclusions about the social efficiency of private decision making that were discussed in Chapter 3. However, in the private sector, an attempt by a subset of a given set of decision makers (say, firms) to form a coalition that moved the economy inside the utility frontier would provide both the possibility and the motivation for new entrants to undercut the coalition and keep the economy on the utility frontier. There is no phenomenon analogous to free entry in the political decision-making process.

20. Important references are Stigler, *The Citizen and the State*; Buchanan and Tullock, *Calculus of Consent*; Borcherding, *Budgets and Governments*; and many papers in the *Journal of Law and Economics*. Chapter 8 of Stigler's work contains a succinct analysis, which although presented in the context of regulation, applies equally well to government spending.

21. Mancur Olson, *The Rise and Decline of Nations* (New Haven, Conn.: Yale University Press, 1982).

22. Olson, *Rise and Decline of Nations*, pp. 148–49.

23. See the survey by Charles Goetz in Borcherding, *Budgets and Governments*.

24. William Niskanen, *Bureaucracy and Representative Government* (Hawthorne,

N.Y.: Aldine, 1971); Tullock, *Private Wants, Public Means*; and Borcherding, *Budgets and Governments.*

25. Niskanen, *Bureaucracy and Representative Government.*

26. Many books and articles by legal specialists debate the pros and cons of social activism among judges. For a superb scholarly account, see Raoul Berger, *Government by Judiciary* (Cambridge, Mass.: Harvard University Press, 1977).

27. See William Doebele, ed., *Land Readjustment* (Lexington, Mass.: Heath, 1982), for discussion of "land readjustment" programs, a euphemism for government confiscation of land as a requirement for permission to develop the land for urban uses. Land readjustment may be good or bad depending on exactly how it works. That is not the issue here. The point is that it is a mechanism under which much of the government cost of providing services for urban development—water, sewage, education, and so forth—is paid for without levying taxes and possibly without appearing on the government budget. Land readjustment is employed in many East Asian countries. In other countries, India for example, governments can freeze rural land prices several years before taking possession of the land, which is then sold to approved developers for urban use. With even a moderate rate of inflation, this procedure transfers most of the value from the farmers from whom the land was bought by eminent domain to the government. See Planning Commission, Task Forces on Housing and Urban Development, *Planning of Urban Development* (New Delhi: Government of India, 1983), pp. 248–52. The government's capital gains may be used in ways that do not show up on the budget.

28. See Edwin Mills and Charles Becker, "Urbanization, Public Services, and Income Distribution in Developing Countries," in B. Prantilla, ed., *National Development and Regional Policy* (Singapore: Maruzen Asia for the U.N. Center for Regional Development, 1981), pp. 57–70, and references therein. It is uncertain to what extent government policies account for the greater inequality in poor than rich countries.

CHAPTER 10

1. Figures in this paragraph are from U.S. Council of Economic Advisers, *Economic Report to the President* (Washington, D.C.: U.S. Government Printing Office, 1984).

2. Figures in this paragraph are from Tax Foundation, Inc., *Facts and Figures on Government Finance* (Washington, D.C.: Tax Foundation, 1983).

3. These figures are a little, but not much, better if one stops in 1980 instead of 1982.

Bibliography

Aaron, Henry. *Politics and the Professors*. Washington, D.C.: Brookings Institution, 1978.

Aaron, Henry, and Boskin, Michael, eds. *The Economics of Taxation*. Washington, D.C.: Brookings Institution, 1980.

Adelman, Irma, and Morris, Cynthia Taft. *Society, Politics, and Economic Development*. Baltimore, Md.: Johns Hopkins University Press, 1967.

Arrow, Kenneth. *The Limits of Organization*. New York: Norton, 1974.

Baghwati, Jagdish, and Desai, Padma. *India: Planning for Industrialization*. London: Oxford University Press, 1970.

Baumol, William. "Macroeconomics of Unbalanced Growth: The Anatomy of the Urban Crisis." *American Economic Review* 57 (June 1967): 415–26.

Baumol, William, and McLennan, Kenneth, eds. *Stimulating U.S. Productivity Growth*. New York: Oxford University Press, 1985.

Baumol, William; Panzer, John; and Willig, Robert. *Contestable Markets and the Theory of Industry Structure*. New York: Harcourt Brace Jovanovich, 1982.

Berger, Raoul. *Government by Judiciary*. Cambridge, Mass.: Harvard University Press, 1977.

Borcherding, Thomas, ed. *Budgets and Governments: Sources of Government Growth*. Durham, N.C.: Duke University Press, 1977

Breton, Albert. *The Economic Theory of Representative Government*. London: Macmillan, 1974.

Buchanan, James. *Freedom in Constitutional Contract: Perspectives of a Political Economist*. College Station: Texas A & M Press, 1978.

Buchanan, James, and Tullock, Gordon. *The Calculus of Consent.* Ann Arbor: University of Michigan Press, 1962.

Buchanan, James, and Wagner, R. E. *Democracy in Deficit.* Orlando, Fla.: Academic Press, 1977.

Buchanan, James, et al. *The Economics of Politics.* London: Institute of Economic Affairs, 1978.

Cameron, David. "The Expansion of the Public Economy: A Comparative Analysis." *American Political Science Review* 72 (1978): 1243–2161.

Coase, Ronald. "The Problem of Social Cost." *Journal of Law and Economics* 3 (October 1960): 1–44.

Congressional Quarterly. *Federal Regulatory Directory, 1983–84.* Washington, D.C.: Congressional Quarterly, 1983.

Council of State Governments, *Book of the States*, vol. 24, 1982–83. Lexington, Ky.: Council of State Governments, 1982.

Crecine, John; Davis, Otto; and Jackson, John. "Urban Property Markets: Some Empirical Results and Their Implications for Municipal Zoning." *Journal of Law and Economics* 10 (1967): 29–100.

Danziger, Sheldon; Haveman, Robert; and Plotnick, Robert. "How Income Transfers Affect Work, Savings, and the Income Distribution." *Journal of Economic Literature* 19, no. 3 (September 1981): 975–1028.

Demsetz, Harold. "Why Regulate Utilities?" *Journal of Law and Economics* 11 (April 1968): 55–65.

Doebele, William, ed. *Land Readjustment.* Lexington, Mass.: Heath, 1982.

Downs, Anthony. *An Economic Theory of Democracy.* New York: Harper, 1957.

———. *Inside Bureaucracy.* Boston: Little, Brown, 1967.

Dunkerley, Harold, ed. *Urban Land Policy.* New York: Oxford University Press, 1983.

Fair, Ray. "The Optimal Distribution of Income." *Quarerly Journal of Economics* 85, no. 4 (November 1971): 551–79.

Feldman, Allan. *Welfare Economics and Social Choice Theory.* Boston: Martinus Nijhoff, 1980.

Friedman, Lawrence. *A History of American Law.* New York: Simon & Schuster, 1973.

Friedman, Milton, and Friedman, Rose. *Free to Choose.* San Diego, Calif.: Harcourt Brace Jovanovich, 1980.

Galbraith, J. Kenneth. *The New Industrial State.* Boston: Houghton Mifflin, 1967.

Garfinkel, Irwin, ed. *Income-Tested Transfer Programs.* Orlando, Fla.: Academic Press, 1982.

Gillis, Malcolm; Perkins, Dwight; Roemer, Michael; and Snodgress, Donald. *Economics of Development.* New York: Norton, 1983.

Hagler, Thomas, ed. "Land Use and Housing in the San Francisco Peninsula."

Stanford Environmental Law Annual 4 (1982). Stanford, Calif.: Stanford Environmental Law Society, 1983.

Haveman, Robert, and Margolis, Julius, eds. *Public Expenditure and Policy Analysis*. Boston: Houghton Mifflin, 1983.

Hochman, Harold. "The Over-Regulated City: A Perspective on Regulatory Procedures in New York City." *Public Finance Quarterly* 9, no. 2 (April 1981): 197, 219.

Hughes, Jonathan. *The Governmental Habit*. New York: Basic Books, 1977.

Intrilligator, Michael, ed., *Frontiers of Quantitative Economics*, Vol. 3. Amsterdam: North-Holland, 1974.

Johnson, Arthur. *Corporate-Business Relations*. Westerville, Ohio: Merrill, 1965.

Jones, E. *The European Miracle*. Cambridge, Eng.: Cambridge University Press, 1981.

Just, Richard; Heuth, Darrell; and Schmitz, Andrew. *Applied Welfare Economics and Public Policy*. Englewood Cliffs, N.J.: Prentice-Hall, 1982.

King, Timothy, ed. *Education and Income*. Staff Working Paper No. 402. Washington, D.C.: World Bank, 1980.

Kramer, Gerald. "Theories of Political Processes." In Intrilligator, Michael, ed., *Frontiers of Quantitative Economics*, Vol. 3. Amsterdam: North-Holland, 1974.

Kravis, Irving; Heston, Alan; and Summers, Robert. *World Production and Income*. Baltimore, Md.: Johns Hopkins University Press, 1982.

Krueger, Anne. *Foreign Trade Regimes and Economic Development: Liberalization Attempts and Consequences*. Cambridge, Mass.: Ballinger, 1978.

Lerner, Abba. *The Economics of Control*. New York: Macmillan, 1944.

Lin, Steven, ed. *Theory and Measurement of Economic Externalities*. Orlando, Fla.: Academic Press, 1976.

Linn, Johannes. *Cities in the Developing World*. New York: Oxford University Press for the World Bank, 1983.

Lippincott, Benjamin, ed. *On the Economic Theory of Socialism*. Minneapolis: University of Minnesota Press, 1948.

Macavoy, Paul, and Sloss, James. *Regulation of Transport Innovation*. New York: Random House, 1963.

McNeill, William. *A World History*. New York: Oxford University Press, 1979.

———. *The Human Condition*. Princeton, N.J.: Princeton University Press, 1980.

———. *The Pursuit of Power*. Chicago: University of Chicago Press, 1982.

Meltzer, Allan, and Richard, Scott. "A Rational Theory of the Size of Government." *Journal of Political Economy* 69, no. 5 (October 1981): 914–27.

Mills, Edwin, and Graves, Philip. *The Economics of Environmental Quality*. New York: Norton, 1986.

Mills, Edwin, and Becker, Charles. "Urbanization, Public Services, and Income Distribution in Developing Countries." In *National Development and Regional*

Policy, edited by B. Prantilla. Singapore: Maruzen Asia for the U.N. Center for Regional Development, 1981.

Mirrlees, James. "Arguments for Public Expenditure." In *Contemporary Economic Analysis*, edited by M. J. Artis and A. R. Nobay. London: Croom Helm, 1978.

Mueller, Dennis. *Public Choice*. Cambridge, Eng.: Cambridge University Press, 1979.

Murray, Charles. *Losing Ground*. New York: Basic Books, 1984.

Myrdal, Gunnar. *Asian Drama*. New York: Twentieth Century Fund, 1968.

National Science Board. *Science Indicators 1980*. Washington, D.C.: National Science Foundation, 1981.

Niskanen, William. *Bureaucracy and Representative Government*. Hawthorne, N.Y.: Aldine, 1971.

North, Douglass. *Structure and Change in Economic History*. New York: Norton, 1981.

North, Douglass, and Thomas, Robert. *The Rise of the Western World*. Cambridge, England: Cambridge University Press, 1973.

Nozick, Robert. *Anarchy, State, and Utopia*. New York: Basic Books, 1974.

Nutter, G. Warren. *Growth of Government in the West*. Washington, D.C.: American Enterprise Institute, 1978.

Okun, Arthur. *Equality and Efficiency: The Big Tradeoff*. Washington, D.C.: Brookings Institution, 1975.

―――. *Prices and Quantities*. Washington, D.C.: Brookings Institution, 1981.

Olson, Mancur. *The Logic of Collective Action*. Cambridge, Mass.: Harvard University Press, 1971.

―――. *The Rise and Decline of Nations*. New Haven, Conn.: Yale University Press, 1981.

Organization for Economic Cooperation and Development. *National Accounts Statistics, 1968–1980*. Paris: Organization for Economic Cooperation and Development, 1982.

Peltzman, Sam. "An Evaluation of Consumer Protection Legislation: The 1962 Drug Amendments." *Journal of Political Economy* 81, no. 5 (September–October 1973): 1049–91.

―――. "The Growth of Government." *Journal of Law and Economics* 23, no. 2 (October 1980): 209–88.

Peskin, Henry; Portney, Paul; and Kneese, Allen, eds. *Environmental Regulation and the U.S. Economy*. Baltimore, Md.: Johns Hopkins University Press for Resources for the Future, 1981.

Planning Commission, Task Forces on Housing and Urban Development. *Planning of Urban Development*. New Delhi: Government of India, 1983.

Rawls, John. *A Theory of Justice*. Cambridge, Mass.: Belknap Press of the Harvard University Press, 1971.

Riker, William, and Ordeshook, Peter. *An Introduction to Positive Political Theory.* Englewood Cliffs, N.J.: Prentice-Hall, 1973.

Satterthwaite, M. A. "Strategy-Proofness and Arrow's Conditions: Existence and Correspondence Theorems for Voting Procedures and Social Welfare Functions." *Journal of Economic Theory* 10 (1975): 182–213.

Seigan, Bernard. *Economic Liberties and the Constitution.* Chicago: University of Chicago Press, 1980.

Sekhar, Uday. *Industrial Location Policy: The Indian Experience.* Staff Working Paper No. 620. Washington, D.C.: World Bank, 1983.

Sen, A. K. *Collective Choice and Social Welfare.* Oakland, Calif.: Holden-Day, 1970.

Slemrod, Joel. "Do We Know How Progressive the Income Tax System Should Be?" *National Tax Journal* 36, no. 3 (1983): 361–69.

Singh, I. J. *Small Farmers and the Landless in South Asia.* Washington, D.C.: World Bank, 1982. Mimeo.

Smith, James, ed. *The Personal Distribution of Income and Wealth.* New York: Columbia University Press for the National Bureau of Economic Research, 1975.

Stern, N. "On the Specification of Models of Optimum Income Taxation." *Journal of Public Economics* 6 (July–August 1976): 123–62.

Stigler, George. *The Citizen and the State.* Chicago: University of Chicago Press, 1975.

Tax Foundation, Inc., *Facts and Figures on Government Finance.* Washington, D.C.: Tax Foundation, 1983.

Taylor, Charles L., ed. *Why Governments Grow.* Beverly Hills, Calif.: Sage, 1983.

Taylor, Charles L., and Jodice, David. *World Handbook of Political and Social Indicators.* New Haven, Conn.: Yale University Press, 1983.

Taylor, Michael. *Anarchy and Cooperation.* New York: Wiley, 1976.

Thurow, Lester. "The Income Redistribution as a Pure Public Good." *Quarterly Journal of Economics* 85, no. 2 (May 1971): 327–36.

Tiebout, Charles. "A Pure Theory of Local Public Expenditures." *Journal of Political Economy* 64 (1956): 416–24.

Todaro, Michael. *Economic Development in the Third World.* New York: Longman, 1981.

Tullock, Gordon. *Private Wants, Public Means.* New York: Basic Books, 1970.

———. *The Social Dilemma.* Blacksburg, Va.: Center for the Study of Public Choice, 1974.

U.S. Census Bureau. *Current Population Reports.* Series P-60, no. 137, March 1983. Washington, D.C.: U.S. Department of Commerce, 1983.

———. *Historical Statistics of the United States.* Washington, D.C.: U.S. Government Printing Office, 1975.

————. *Statistical Abstract of the United States 1982–83.* Washington, D.C.: U.S. Government Printing Office, 1984.

U.S. Council of Economic Advisers. *Economic Report to the President.* Washington, D.C.: U.S. Government Printing Office, annual.

U.S. Internal Revenue Service. *Statistics of Income, Personal Income Tax Returns, 1980.* Washington, D.C.: U.S. Department of Justice, 1983.

Usher, Dan. *The Economic Prerequisites of Democracy.* New York: Columbia University Press, 1981.

Weidenbaum, Murray. *Business, Government, and the Public.* Englewood Cliffs, N.J.: Prentice-Hall, 1981.

White, Lawrence. *Reforming Regulation.* Englewood Cliffs, N.J.: Prentice-Hall, 1981.

Williamson, Jeffrey, and Lindert, Peter. *American Inequality.* Orlando, Fla.: Academic Press, 1980.

World Bank. *World Tables.* 3d ed. Baltimore, Md.: Johns Hopkins University Press, 1983.

————. *World Development Report 1984.* New York: Oxford University Press, 1984.

Wright, Nancy, and Allen, Gene. *National Directory of State Agencies, 1982–1983.* Arlington, Va.: Information Resources Press, 1982.

Yotopoulos, P., and Nugent, J. *Economics of Development: Empirical Investigations.* New York: Harper & Row, 1976.

Zodrow, George, ed. *Local Provision of Public Services: The Tiebout World After Twenty-Five Years.* Orlando, Fla.: Academic Press, 1983.

Index